Second Helpings

Delicious Dishes to Transform Your Leftovers

Sue Quinn

Photography by Facundo Bustamante

QUADRILLE

6

Introduction

Leftovers. It's not the most tantalizing way to describe the remains of a meal (the French have a lovelier expression – *les restes*). In fact, the term 'leftovers' does a disservice to perfectly good food by implying that it's somehow second-rate or less delicious than it was on its first outing to the table. To my mind, nothing could be further from the truth.

According to some historians, the concept of 'leftovers' didn't even exist until domestic refrigerators became more commonplace around the turn of the 20th century. Before then, leftovers were just food. Much-loved dishes like cottage or shepherd's pie were simply ways of using up what remained of a Sunday roast; bread and butter pudding was a delicious solution for stale bread. And because all food was precious and highly valued, uneaten portions were preserved by processes such as salting, drying, pickling or smoking – all part and parcel of everyday food preparation. 'Leftovers' only became a food genre when chilling made it possible to delay spoiling.

In the early 20th century, thrift in the kitchen was not only necessary for many people – particularly in view of years of food shortages during two world wars and the Great Depression – but widely regarded as morally right. Some cookbooks were dedicated to this 'new' culinary category, others were sprinkled with handy tips for repurposing scraps from the dishes readers made. By the 1960s, attitudes began to shift and love for leftovers dimmed. In fact, binning leftovers became a gaudy way to demonstrate how comfortably middle class you were. Recycling last night's dinner was the butt of jokes.

To some extent, leftovers are still tainted by that terrible, wasteful view. But sky-rocketing food prices, the climate-change crisis and world events that threaten food security are forcing us to reassess our thinking. And for so many reasons this is welcome news. For a start, leftovers are often tastier than the original meal because the various ingredients have had a chance to cosy up and for the flavours to develop. What's more, it's an efficient approach to preparing meals. Using food that is already cooked saves time because you've done much of the work already. In fact, I now deliberately generate leftovers wherever I can, and make double (or more) than I need. It just makes so much sense. If I'm switching on the oven, why not roast several trays of vegetables instead of just one, to save time, energy and create future meals? If I'm stirring a pot of risotto for 20 minutes, it's no extra effort to make double.

Leftovers are inspiring, too. Even those of us who love cooking struggle to come up with fresh ideas for meals on a daily basis. But framing a dish around food that needs using up is a helpful guide, and you don't need a whole plate of Sunday roast leftovers to do this. Milk that is past its best (use your judgement on that) can lead you to a luscious chicken dish (see page 102). Past-their-prime oddments in the crisper drawer can become the launchpad for a comforting pie (see pages 16–21). The bones and juices from a roast chicken are the base for a tasty soup or stock (see pages 32–35), while even used grounds from your daily coffee can be turned into cookies (see page 161).

I find using up random scraps of food an exciting and satisfying way to cook. Years ago, when I was flat-sharing, our household had a fine old time playing 'ready, steady, cook' with the slim pickings lurking in the fridge and kitchen cupboard. I hope you will gain the confidence to similarly improvise and experiment beyond the scope of the actual recipes in this book. Once you're in the leftovers mindset, it's not hard. Start by corralling on your worktop what needs using up and assess what you have. The end of a pot of cream? Simmer with a spoonful or two of cooked chopped vegetables (frozen peas would do), a cup of stock and some added flavours (herbs, spices, garlic and so on) for a fine sauce for pasta. A handful of things left from last night's dinner? It doesn't really matter what you have, just chop it small, then fold into pancake batter or beaten eggs for an omelette. Dinner done.

It's not for me to lecture on the wider benefits of reducing food waste – this book is about elevating leftovers into dishes that are exciting and inviting. But a few facts are worth sharing. It's estimated that almost a billion tonnes of food are thrown out every year across the world. As well as being financially foolish, wasting food damages the planet because it accelerates climate change. The initial food-production journey from farm to plate produces greenhouse gases, with more created whenever we throw uneaten food away, as a vast amount of methane is produced while our wasted food slowly rots in landfill.

It's never been more important to use up and enjoy all the food we buy, so I've included recipes that feature commonly binned ingredients, as well as leftover cooked food. These unused 'leftovers' – chucked because they're past their best or surplus to immediate needs – include bread, milk, cheese, salad leaves, potatoes, bananas, apples, other fruit and veg and the remains of takeaways. Trust your eyes, nose and common sense to decide whether fruit, veg or store-cupboard ingredients really are only good until the best-before date on the packaging.

I prefer to view leftovers as potentially delicious future meals rather than using them up as being a worthy act. Second helpings are an opportunity too good to waste.

Cook's Notes

Butter: unless stated otherwise, use whatever you have, either salted or unsalted.

Salt: expensive flaked salt is wasted in cooking, so I've used fine sea salt throughout and specified flaked only where it's really needed.

Cook and prep times: preparation time includes ingredient prep and whatever cooking needs to be constantly monitored. Cooking includes baking, roasting and time on the hob when food can be left unattended.

Safety note:

You should always chill leftover rice as quickly as possible, ideally within 1 hour. When reheated, it must be steaming hot all the way through. Rice shouldn't be reheated more than once, so if using takeaway rice, ask if it was cooked from scratch in the first place.

Master Recipes

Pasta bake

LEFTOVERS

Odds and ends of cooked and uncooked vegetables, pasta, herbs,
leftover cooked chicken, turkey, ham, beef, lamb or vegetarian sausages

Who doesn't love a pasta bake? It's such an adaptable dish and a fantastic vehicle for all kinds of savoury leftovers.

I've offered two pasta bake options: one with tomato sauce and a creamy version. (The latter is much lighter than a standard cheese sauce.) Both start from the same base recipe below and then veer off in separate directions overleaf.

Base recipe

Serves 4–6
Preparation: up to 40 minutes
Cooking: about 30 minutes

For the base
300g (10½oz) uncooked or 600g (1lb 5oz) cooked pasta (or a mixture but keep cooked and uncooked separate), any shape
1 Tbsp olive oil, plus an extra splash
1 onion or 1 small leek, finely sliced
3 garlic cloves, grated
1 tsp dried oregano or mixed herbs
1 tsp chilli flakes
3 smoked bacon rashers (strips), chopped, or a handful of lardons (optional)
700g (1lb 9oz) uncooked or cooked vegetables (or a mixture but keep cooked and uncooked separate), chopped small
Fine sea salt and freshly ground black pepper

Start by cooking the pasta (unless using leftover cooked pasta). Cook in salted boiling water for a minute less than the packet instructions. Drain, toss with a splash of olive oil and set aside.

Meanwhile, warm the tablespoon of olive oil in a large frying pan (skillet), and gently fry the onion with a pinch of salt until soft and translucent, 8–10 minutes. Add the garlic, herbs and chilli flakes and fry for 2 minutes, stirring.

Add the bacon (if using) and any sturdy uncooked veg such as roots, cauliflower, broccoli or pumpkin. Stir-fry over a medium heat for a few minutes. Reduce the heat to low, add a splash of water and cover. Cook, stirring now and then to prevent sticking, until almost tender. Add a splash more water as needed.

Add any soft vegetables or leafy greens and cook until just tender.

Now pick either a tomato or white sauce for your pasta bake overleaf.

Tomato sauce pasta bake

White sauce pasta bake

2 x 400g (14oz) cans chopped tomatoes
1 Tbsp tomato purée (paste)
Fine sea salt
A handful of cooked meat or meat alternative, shredded, or vegetarian sausages or 1 x 160g (5¾oz) can of tuna, drained
About 200g (7oz) grated cheese, a mix of whatever you have (a mozzarella ball in there is lovely but not essential)

Preheat the oven to 190°C/170°C fan/375°F/Gas mark 5. Tip the canned tomatoes into the pan with the cooked base ingredients and add a generous pinch of salt. Stir in the tomato purée (paste) and simmer gently until the tomatoes have thickened into a sauce.

Stir in the cooked meat (if using), cooked vegetables and the cooked pasta.

Tip into a large baking dish, scatter over the grated cheese and dot with mozzarella (if using). Bake for about 25–30 minutes, or until golden and bubbling.

1 x 160g (5¾oz) can tuna, drained (optional)
4 Tbsp butter
4 Tbsp plain (all-purpose) flour
400ml (1¾ cups) strong chicken or vegetable stock
200ml (scant 1 cup) double (heavy) cream
200g (7oz) grated cheese, a mix of whatever you have (a mozzarella ball in there is lovely but not essential)
¼ tsp grated nutmeg
Fine sea salt and freshly ground black pepper

Preheat the oven to 190°C/170°C fan/375°F/Gas mark 5. Take the pan of cooked base ingredients off the heat, add the cooked pasta and tuna (if using), and mix gently to combine. Set aside while you make the white sauce.

Melt the butter in a medium pan. When foaming, stir in the flour. Cook over a medium heat, stirring constantly, until pale gold. Whisk in the stock and cook over a low heat, stirring, until it thickens.

Take the pan off the heat and stir in the cream, half the grated cheese and the nutmeg. Season generously to taste with salt and pepper.

Stir the sauce into the pasta mixture. Transfer to a large baking dish and scatter over the remaining grated cheese. Bake for 30 minutes or until golden and bubbling.

Pasta bake

Stews *and* pies

LEFTOVERS

Cooked meat and vegetables

Leftovers simmered in a rich and comforting sauce – aka stew – is a meal everyone warms to. And it's flexible. Serve on toast or crumpets for something casual or with mash or polenta when everyone's ravenous. Alternatively, tuck the stew inside a pastry blanket or cover with mash for pie.

Whatever direction you're headed, leftover meat, poultry and vegetables can all go in. If using leftover beef or lamb the rarest bits work best, as they're less likely to toughen with further cooking. Choose the vibe you fancy with the herbs, spices and other flavourings – I've offered ideas, but this is a template and great for experimenting.

A word on pastry: the best pies, in my opinion, have a shortcrust base and a puff pastry top. Shortcrust top and bottom is heavy going and puff on the bottom can go soggy. By all means, leave out the pastry bottom altogether and just use puff or shortcrust on top.

If you do go for double crust, reduce the sauce right down until there's barely any left. Another option is to lift the stew out of the pan with a slotted spoon to drain off almost all of the sauce before transferring it to the pie dish. You can always serve the extra sauce on the side.

Base recipe

*Serves 4 as stew, or makes a
    20cm (8in) pie*
Preparation: up to 45 minutes
*Cooking: 25 minutes for pies with
    pastry top*

Make your base
1 rasher (strip) of bacon or a handful
    of lardons (optional)
2 Tbsp olive oil
1 medium onion or leek, finely
    chopped or sliced
1 carrot, finely chopped
1 celery stick, finely chopped
A good pinch of salt

Heat a large frying pan (skillet) and fry the bacon (if using) until
crisp at the edges. Scoop out and transfer to a plate. Add the oil
and gently fry the onion or leek, carrot and celery until very soft,
10–15 minutes.

Now follow steps 1–8 on these pages and continued overleaf.

1. Add flavour

Add the ingredients below to the cooked base and
fry gently for a few minutes, stirring, to release
the flavour.

- 2 Tbsp tomato purée (paste) or tomato ketchup
  (red meat only)
- 1 fat garlic clove, finely chopped
- 1 bay leaf

2. Boost flavour

Add **one** of the bulleted ingredients below and fry,
stirring for a minute or two, until fragrant.

For red meat
- 1 tsp each ground cinnamon, allspice and
  dried mint
- 1½ Tbsp baharat (see overleaf) or ras el hanout
- 2 tsp dried oregano and 1 tsp smoked paprika
- 2–3 Tbsp red curry paste or powder
- 1 Tbsp chopped fresh rosemary or thyme

For poultry or vegetables
- 1½ Tbsp baharat (see overleaf) or ras el hanout
- 1 Tbsp dried thyme or tarragon
- 1 Tbsp each chopped fresh tarragon and parsley
- 2–3 Tbsp curry paste or powder

3. Thicken

Stir 1 heaped Tbsp of plain (all-purpose) flour into the mixture and cook, stirring, until amalgamated.

4. The sauce

For red meat
Add 300ml (1¼ cups plus 1 Tbsp) red wine plus 300ml (1¼ cups plus 1 Tbsp) beef, chicken or vegetable stock. Stir and gently simmer until reduced by one-third.

For poultry or vegetables
Add 80ml (⅓ cup) white wine and simmer, stirring, until almost evaporated. Add 300ml (1¼ cups plus 1 Tbsp) chicken or vegetable stock plus 300ml (1¼ cups plus 1 Tbsp) double (heavy) cream or crème fraîche. Simmer gently until reduced by one-third.

5. Add your main filling ingredients

Gently stir in your leftovers: 300–400g (10½–14oz) diced cooked meat, poultry or vegetables.

6. Bulk it out

Add one or two of the ingredients below, depending on how much of the main filling ingredients you have. Any uncooked leafy greens you use will release some water during cooking, so be sure to reduce the sauce right down.

- A generous handful of sliced leafy greens such as kale, spinach or chard
- A generous handful of frozen peas
- A generous handful of chopped roast veg
- 1 mug of drained canned cannellini or butter (lima) beans, or cooked green or Puy lentils (great with ras el hanout spicing)
- A handful of chopped walnuts or pistachios if you're using meat, or pine nuts or almonds for poultry

7. Brighten

Take the pan off the heat and stir in one of the ingredients below to brighten the flavour.

Red meat
- Finely grated zest of ½ lemon
- A small handful of dried cherries, cranberries or barberries
- 4 pickled walnuts or 2 Tbsp capers, chopped
- A splash of balsamic vinegar, red wine vinegar or pomegranate molasses

Chicken or veg
- Finely grated zest of ½ lemon
- 1–2 tsp Dijon mustard
- 1 Tbsp capers, chopped

8. Serve

For stew
Serve hot with mashed potatoes, rice, polenta or on toast or crumpets.

For pie
1 sheet ready-rolled shortcrust pastry (optional, for the base)
1 sheet ready-rolled puff pastry or mashed potato (for the top)
1 lightly beaten egg
2 Tbsp butter (for mash top)

Set the stew aside to cool a little and preheat the oven to 200°C/180°C fan/400°F/Gas mark 6. If you want pastry top and bottom, slide a baking sheet into the oven to heat up. Line a 20cm (8in) pie dish with ready-rolled shortcrust. Trim the edges and brush with lightly beaten egg. If you're not having a pastry base, just brush the edge of the pie dish with some of the egg.

Once the oven is hot, spoon the stew into the dish. For a pastry top, top with the sheet of puff pastry, press the edges onto the pastry base or pie dish and trim off the excess. Brush with the remaining beaten egg and make a couple of slits in the top with a knife. Slide onto the hot baking sheet and bake according to the packet instructions, or until golden.

For a mashed potato top, cover generously with mashed potato and dot with the butter. Bake until hot and bubbling.

To make the North African spice blend **baharat** mix together 1 Tbsp each ground cumin, coriander, black pepper and paprika. This quantity is more than you need for this recipe, so store the rest in a sealed jar.

Vegetables

LEFTOVERS

Odds and ends of vegetables

Whether left over from a Sunday roast, lurking past their prime in the salad crisper drawer or you just have too many to use up before they spoil, surplus veg offer loads of possibilities.

Cooked veg ideas

It's tempting to throw away the odd scoopful of cooked veg, but even apparently unusable amounts can be souped up into something delicious.

1. Crostini or sandwiches make a great home for them. Chop the veg small and mix with flavour accessories such as: grated strong cheese (Parmesan, Cheddar, crumbled feta or blue); finely chopped olives, anchovies, capers or pickles; chopped fresh herbs; a sprinkling of dried herbs like oregano and mint; or a spoonful of chilli paste or oil.Squish generous spoonfuls of this mixture onto hot toast spread with butter, hummus, labneh or whipped feta. Or stuff between slices of bread slicked with mayo for sandwiches – fry these in butter for toasties if you fancy.

2. Cooked chopped veg are terrific in omelettes. Pour 6–8 beaten eggs into a 20cm (8in) frying pan (skillet) – or use just 3 eggs for a thin open omelette. Cook gently until the egg is almost set. For a folded omelette, spread cooked veg and some grated cheese over one half, then fold the other half over, continue cooking for a couple of minutes, then gently slide onto a plate. For an open omelette, scatter the vegetables over the top, sprinkle with grated cheese and finish under the grill (broiler).

3. Leftover cooked greens – spinach, chard, kale or cabbage – are great united with eggs. Melt a knob of butter in a frying pan with a splash of olive oil and a little crushed garlic. When foaming, add the greens and swipe them around the pan to get buttery and garlicky. Shape them into a mound with an indent in the middle and crack an egg into it. Reduce the heat to low, cover the pan with a lid and cook until the egg white is just set. Grated Parmesan on top is lovely.

Past their prime

Less-than-perky uncooked vegetables – including scraps from the salad crisper drawer of the fridge – will serve you well after a stint in a hot oven. All types of veg roast well, just chop everything roughly the same size, toss with olive oil and sprinkle with salt. Spread out in a large roasting tray – avoid overcrowding. Add a head of garlic, sliced in half horizontally, and drizzle with oil. Roast at 200°C/180°C fan/400°F/Gas mark 6 until tender and slightly browned at the edges, about 45 minutes depending on size and type of vegetables. Check on the veg occasionally and scoop them out as they finish cooking – root veg will take longer than things like (bell) peppers and courgettes (zucchini).

Use the roasted veg in the braise (see right), in recipes throughout the book or on their own served with roasted garlic yoghurt. For this, simply squeeze the roasted garlic cloves into 150g (¾ cup) of Greek yoghurt, add salt and stir.

Braised

You can make a quick braise with cooked veg. Heat some olive oil in a frying pan (skillet) and fry a finely chopped onion until soft and translucent. Add a couple of chopped garlic cloves and a good pinch of chilli flakes and fry for 2 minutes more. Add a can of chopped tomatoes and 200ml (scant 1 cup) vegetable or chicken stock. Simmer gently until reduced to a thick sauce. Stir through some cooked veg and cook gently to warm through. Serve with mashed potato or polenta (stir through a spoonful of mascarpone for extra richness) or use as a pasta sauce.

For a super-simple soup (see more soup ideas on pages 32–35), bring 400ml (1¾ cups) vegetable or chicken stock to the boil in a medium pan. Stir in 1 Tbsp miso paste, curry paste or chilli paste (like gochujang). Reduce to a simmer, then add leftover chopped cooked vegetables and cook gently until warmed through. Serve with chopped spring onions (scallions), a splash of soy sauce and/or finely sliced seaweed; hard-boiled egg halves; or a swirl of soured cream, crème fraîche or Greek yoghurt.

Risotto

LEFTOVERS

Cooked and uncooked vegetables,
cooked meat or chicken, odds and ends of cheese

I can't think of any savoury leftover ingredients that can't take a star turn in the risotto pot. This recipe comes into its own to use up leftovers after Christmas, Thanksgiving or on Monday after a Sunday roast. But any time is good for risotto.

Risotto components

Stock
By all means use shop-bought stock or stock (bouillon) cubes; I often do. But if you have a turkey or chicken carcass hanging about, making your own is really no effort and more delicious. Place the carcass and any bones from people's plates (don't worry, they're going to be cooked for hours) in a large stockpot. Add a carrot, celery stick and onion (all chopped in half) plus a few bay leaves and a few peppercorns. Cover with water by a good few centimetres (an inch) and simmer on the lowest heat for 2–3 hours. Drain through a colander (strainer), return the stock to the pot and simmer until reduced and full of flavour. Add salt to taste. Use for the Essential risotto overleaf or freeze for later.

Cheese
Parmesan is traditionally stirred into risotto at the end of cooking for creaminess and extra umami oomph. But almost any cheese works well. Use a mixture of cheeseboard leftovers, or any chunk that needs using up. If you use a strong cheese, like a blue, be judicious, so as not to overpower. One option is to leave whiffy cheese on the side for guests to crumble over as they wish.

Vegetables
Any leftover vegetables can be stirred into risotto, including potatoes. Remember that if you use lots of beetroot (beet), the resulting dish will be Barbie-pink but still taste great. I've suggested using small chunks of vegetables but another idea is to whizz some of the veg into a purée and stir through the cooked rice.

Meat
Any leftover meat or meat alternative works in risotto: chopped or shredded beef, lamb, pork, bacon, chicken or turkey, and vegetarian sausages. Make sure the meat is piping hot before serving.

Grains
Pearl barley works beautifully to make 'risotto' (in Italy it's called orzotto). It will take a little longer to cook and you might have to adjust the amount of stock you use. At a pinch you can also use long-grain rice, such as basmati, but don't rinse it first.

Essential risotto recipe

Serves 6

Preparation: about 30 minutes, plus 5 minutes to 'rest'

1.5 litres (6½ cups) chicken, turkey or vegetable stock
75g (2½oz) unsalted butter
1 Tbsp olive oil
1 onion, very finely chopped
450g (generous 2¼ cups) Arborio or Carnaroli rice
100ml (scant ½ cup) white wine
A good handful of cooked chicken, turkey, ham or sausages, cut into small pieces (optional) and/or chopped cooked vegetables
A handful of grated or crumbled cheese
Fine sea salt and freshly ground black pepper

Pour the stock into a pan and keep it hot but not boiling over low heat.

Melt 2 tablespoons of the butter and the tablespoon of oil in a heavy pan and gently fry the onion with a pinch of salt until soft and translucent, about 8 minutes. Add the rice and stir to coat in the buttery oil. Cook over a medium heat for 2 minutes, stirring, to toast.

Stir in the wine and, once evaporated, start adding the stock a ladleful at a time, stirring between each addition. Wait until one ladleful of stock has almost evaporated before adding more.

After 15 minutes, add the leftover meat (if using) and vegetables. Continue adding stock as before until the rice is tender but still retains some bite.

Take the pan off the heat and gently stir in the remaining butter and the cheese. Cover and set aside for 5 minutes. Taste for seasoning, adding more salt and pepper if needed. Serve immediately.

Hash and Bubble *and* squeak

LEFTOVERS

Cooked vegetables, cooked meat, takeaway chips,
odds and ends of herbs, chilli paste, cooked pasta

Both these variations on a theme are, deservedly, irresistible classics: quick to cook, deeply satisfying and scrumptious in a different way every time you make them.

Bubble and squeak generally involves mashing everything up – I pulse the ingredients in the food processer until roughly combined (don't blitz until smooth or you will end up with an unappealing paste). In hash, everything is left in chunks, so it's more of a rough and tumble affair. Potatoes are essential in both dishes – they stick everything together.

If you don't have enough leftover cooked veg, top up with frozen peas, or I've added a scoop or two of leftover pasta and sauce with no regrets. Leftover takeaway chips? Add those too.

Serves 2–4
Preparation: 5 minutes
Cooking: 20 minutes

600–700g (1lb 5oz–1lb 9oz) cooked chopped veg
A handful of chopped or shredded cooked meat (optional)
Chopped fresh herbs such as parsley or chives, chopped (optional)
1 Tbsp dripping, the fat from your roast, duck, goose or bacon fat, or olive oil
1 Tbsp butter
A handful of grated cheese (optional)
Lots of salt and pepper

If you're making bubble and squeak, mash the vegetables together or pulse in a food processor until roughly combined. For hash, leave the veg pieces chunky and mash lightly with a potato masher.

Stir in any meat or herbs you fancy using up.

Heat the fat or oil and butter in a 20cm (8in) frying pan (skillet), preferably one with an ovenproof handle. When hot, add the veg. Press the veg into the sizzling fat and cook over a medium-high heat for 5 minutes or so until golden underneath. Turn the vegetables over as they crisp up and flatten gently with an egg slice. Repeat until everything is hot with crunchy bits incorporated.

Sprinkle with cheese (if using) and pop under the grill (broiler) until golden and bubbling. Serve immediately.

Try...
Topping the finished dish with a fried egg.

Adding finely chopped garlic, 1 Tbsp chilli paste (harissa, gochujang and chipotle work beautifully) and/or 1 Tbsp ras el hanout to the mixture before frying.

Soup

LEFTOVERS

Cooked and uncooked vegetables, cooked meat, odds and ends of cheese and cheese rinds, stale bread, ends of jars of chilli paste, ends of tubs of cream, crème fraîche or soured cream

Soup is the perfect vehicle for oddments of uncooked and cooked veg and/or meat. Decide whether you fancy a brothy soup similar to minestrone or ribollita, or a thicker, puréed soup. Then, make your own adventure, as they say, according to what you've got.

This is just a guide: double up the quantities suggested here if you have lots of ingredients to use up. It freezes well.

Base recipe

Serves 4
Preparation: up to 40 minutes, depending on the veg

For the base
A handful of chopped bacon, pancetta or guanciale (optional)
3 Tbsp olive oil
1 onion or leek (white part), finely chopped
Fine sea salt
1 celery stick, finely chopped
1 fat garlic clove, finely chopped
½ Tbsp chopped fresh rosemary or thyme

Add the bacon (if using) to a large pan set over medium heat and fry until starting to crisp at the edges. Reduce the heat to medium-low, add the oil and fry the onion or leek and celery with a pinch of salt until very soft and translucent, about 10–15 minutes. Add the garlic and herbs and cook for a couple of minutes more.

Now pick from either a brothy or pureed soup overleaf.

Brothy soup

1 Tbsp tomato purée (paste)
1.5 litres (6½ cups) chicken or vegetable stock
(or more or less as needed)
1 Parmesan rind (optional but very tasty)
A spoonful of pesto (optional)

For brothy soup
Stir the tomato purée (paste) into the base mixture and fry for a minute or two. Then add the stock and Parmesan rind (if using).

Add your choice of the following – just make sure the ingredients are completely covered by stock. If you're using uncooked vegetables, add these first and cook until tender. Pasta (if using) goes in next. Add any canned chickpeas (garbanzo beans) or beans, cooked veg or meat at the end and simmer gently until warmed through.

- Uncooked sturdy vegetables such as pumpkin, potato, carrots, swede (rutabaga) or cauliflower, cut into small cubes
- Tiny pasta – orzo or stars – or broken-up fine pasta
- Canned chickpeas (garbanzo beans) or white beans or leftover cooked vegetables, chopped small
- Shredded or chopped meat or poultry

Once everything is warmed through, take the pan off the heat and add any finely sliced greens such as kale, chard or lettuce to wilt in the residual heat. Stir in a spoonful of pesto (if using). Add more hot stock if necessary to make it more brothy.

Puréed soup

A couple of good handfuls of sturdy uncooked vegetables such as pumpkin, potato, carrots, swede (rutabaga), cauliflower or a combination, cut into small cubes
1.5 litres (6½ cups) chicken or vegetable stock
(or more or less as needed)
1 Parmesan rind (optional but very tasty)
Cooked vegetables, cut into small cubes
Lemon juice, to taste
Fine sea salt and freshly ground black pepper

Optional
Grated cheese
Soured cream, crème fraîche or cream
A spoonful of chilli paste, such as harissa, chipotle or gochujang

For puréed soup
Add any uncooked veg to the base mixture. Pour in enough stock to cover by several centimetres and add a Parmesan rind (if using). Bring to the boil, then lower the heat and simmer gently until the vegetables are tender. Add any cooked veg and continue cooking until warmed through.

Scoop all the vegetables and some of the liquid into a blender or food processor (I pour the lot into a colander/strainer set over a large jug for this). Blitz until smooth and add enough stock to produce the soup consistency you love. Return the puréed veg to the pot to warm through.

Add a good squeeze of lemon juice, and then taste for seasoning and add more salt and pepper if needed. If you like, stir in a handful of grated cheese, or a spoonful or two of crème fraîche, soured cream or cream, or some chilli paste.

Serving suggestions
Top with grated Parmesan and a drizzle of extra virgin olive oil.

Place a slice of toasted or stale bread in the bottom of the bowls before ladling in the soup.

Fry cubes of stale bread in garlic-infused olive oil and sprinkle over the top.

Sprinkle with chopped fresh herbs.

Salad

LEFTOVERS

Cooked and uncooked vegetables, cooked meat,
half-used packets of nuts, seeds and dried fruit;
ends of jars of condiments, pastes, pickles and preserved lemon

Cold salads are an excellent way to use up oddments from the fridge or store cupboard. The options are endless.

As your benchmark, think of the classic French *salade composée*, that irresistible arrangement of good things on a plate. Raw vegetables (finely sliced or shaved into ribbons), herbs (chopped or use whole just like salad leaves) and fruit can rub shoulders with richer elements like cheese, toasted nuts, eggs, shredded meat or canned fish. Sturdy components like cooked vegetables (potatoes, sweet potato or pumpkin), canned white beans or chickpeas (garbanzo beans), chunks of bread or cold cooked root veg can elevate salad to a filling meal.

Half-used packets of things and jars at the back of the fridge can be plundered, too. Capers, preserved lemon, chilli paste and pickled veg can add punch to a dressing or extra tang on the plate. Nuts and seeds can be toasted and sprinkled over for crunch. I love salads that hide lots of different tiny treasures, so each mouthful is a surprise.

Basic salad recipe

First make the dressing – the longer the flavours mingle, the better it will taste. Basic vinaigrette is zippy, easy and adaptable. I like three or four parts oil (50% extra virgin olive oil, 50% flavourless oil) to one part vinegar/lemon juice, plus a touch of Dijon mustard, crushed garlic, a whisper of honey and lots of salt and pepper. Finely chopped anchovy fillets in oil (drained) or capers add extra punch. Pop everything into a lidded jar and shake. For a creamy version, add a little yoghurt, crème fraîche or mayonnaise. Fresh/dried herbs, ground spices (paprika, chilli flakes, cumin) bolster the flavour too.

Start your salad with a creamy base layer (only if you fancy, it's not obligatory) onto which you will then build. Thick Greek yoghurt or labneh with your choice of finely chopped preserved lemon, garlic, chopped herbs, flaked chilli and/or olive oil swirled through is lovely. Or whizz up equal quantities of feta/goat's cheese and Greek yoghurt with a touch of your favourite chilli paste. Spread a thin layer all over your serving platter – you'll get a luscious creamy element with each scoop of salad.

Leaves and tender raw vegetables come next – a ragtag of sliced or torn lettuce, herbs, cauliflower leaves, cabbage, or Brussels sprouts, for example, is delicious. Past-their-best specimens can be perked up with a soak in cold water, then dried in a salad spinner or clean tea towel (dish towel). Place the leaves in a bowl and add finely shaved or sliced raw veg: carrots, courgette (zucchini), broccoli stalks, radishes, cucumber, celery or fennel bulb. Toss with a little of the dressing and scatter over the creamy base.

Top the leaves and raw veg with clusters of heavier good things: shredded cooked chicken, sliced fresh fruit, chopped dried fruit, cooked vegetables, cheese (spoonfuls of ricotta or slices of hard cheese like Cheddar or Gruyère), halved hard-boiled eggs, canned/jarred white beans or chickpeas (garbanzo beans), cooked grains or canned fish.

Include something sharp or tangy: pickled veg, sauerkraut or kimchi.

Scatter toasted nuts or seeds over the top (try the za'atar roasted seeds on page 96).

Finally, drizzle with some of the remaining dressing and serve immediately.

Fruit

LEFTOVERS

Hard fruit, fruit past its prime, a glut of fruit

There are endless reasons why you could have leftover fruit: it might be hard as a rock and refusing to ripen; or it's overripe and your household is ignoring it; your fruit bowl is spilling over, and you won't get through it all before it starts to turn. Whatever your fruit situation, here are some simple and delicious ways to use it all up. Elsewhere in the book you'll find more detailed recipes for fruity leftovers.

Poach

Rock-hard flavourless fruit can be coaxed into tasty tenderness by gently simmering in a light sugar syrup. Mix one part sugar with two parts water (by weight) in a pan large enough to hold the fruit in a single layer. I use a large frying pan (skillet) to which I add 200g (generous 1 cup) caster (superfine) sugar and 400ml (1¾ cups) water, and simmer until dissolved. Then I add some of the following flavourings: a couple of crushed cardamom pods; a cinnamon stick; lemon or orange peel; sprigs of woody herbs like bay, rosemary, or thyme. You can also replace half the water with wine or add a splash of fruity booze like sherry, Cointreau or muscat.

Once you've made the poaching liquor, add the fruit: halved and stoned peaches, nectarines, plums or apricots (I leave the skin on) or halved and cored pears (quartered if large) all work well. Simmer the fruit until it's tender but still holding its shape – half-cover the pan with a lid if the fruit resists softening – and turn it over in the syrup now and then.

Roast

Any kind of underripe fruit like stone fruit or pears (or apples if you need to use some up) can be roasted. Halve and remove the stones from stone fruit (if the stones won't easily budge, just remove after roasting); core and cut pears/apples lengthways into quarters (or eighths if large). Arrange cut-side up in a roasting tray or baking dish – the fruit needs to fit snugly, or the juices will burn.

Sprinkle with sugar and spice (mixed spice, nutmeg or cinnamon), dot with butter and roast for 30–40 minutes at 190°C/170°C fan/375°F/Gas mark 5, or until the fruit is tender.

Alternatively, instead of sugar and spice, toss the fruit with 2 tablespoons of melted butter mixed with any of the following (this should be enough for one large tray of fruit):

- 2 Tbsp runny honey and ¼ tsp crushed fennel seeds
- 2 Tbsp maple syrup and 1 bay leaf
- 2 Tbsp marmalade
- 2 Tbsp golden syrup, freshly grated ginger (or chopped preserved ginger) and grated lemon zest

Stew

For fruit that's super-soft or overripe, chop into bite-sized chunks and place in a pan with a splash of water, a sprinkling of sugar and a good squeeze of lemon juice. Cook over a medium-low heat, stirring often, until the fruit starts to soften and release its juices. Cook for as long as you like – boil if you want to reduce it to a thick sauce or jam. Taste and add more sugar if you like.

Ideas for cooked fruit

1. Cooked fruit is lovely served simply with ice cream or yoghurt. If you've poached it, spoon over some of the syrup you cooked it in. (Any leftover syrup makes a delicious cordial or add a splash to fizzy water or alcoholic bubbles. The syrup will keep well in the fridge for a week or so.) Or serve the fruit with gently whipped scented cream made by folding through your choice of the following: vanilla seeds scraped from a pod; finely grated orange or lemon zest; orange flower or rose water; fruity liqueur, dessert wine or sherry; a sprinkling of cinnamon and brown sugar.

2. For a super-quick and tasty pudding, serve cooked fruit with sugar-and-spice croutons. Melt a few knobs of butter in a frying pan and, when foaming, add small cubes of bread. Fry over a medium-high heat until golden. Sprinkle with sugar and spice (cinnamon, nutmeg or mixed spice) and fry until caramelized.

3. Poached or roasted fruit makes a fantastic and super-easy tart – the cooking has drawn out the juices, so the risk of a soggy bottom is reduced. Just line a tart case with pastry (puff is best for this but shortcrust works, too). Pack tightly with a single layer of poached or roasted fruit – drain off any syrup or juices clinging to the fruit first. Bake at 220°C/200°C fan/425°F/Gas mark 7 for about 25 minutes or until the pastry is golden. You need 900g–1kg (2–2lb 3oz) of uncooked fruit to fill a 23cm (9in) tart tin.

Fruit on crumpets

This is based on a recipe in Jane Grigson's *Fruit Book* and makes an exceptional snack or pudding.

Preparation: 5 minutes
Cooking: 10 minutes

Preheat the oven to 220°C/200°C fan/425°F/Gas mark 7 and place a baking sheet inside to heat up. Butter both sides of crumpets, place holes-side up on a sheet of foil, and top with slices or pieces of cooked fruit or a spoonful of berries. Drizzle with a little melted butter, sprinkle with sugar and slide onto the hot baking sheet. Bake for 10 minutes or until the bottoms of the crumpets are golden and the tops sizzling. Also good with thick slices of brioche or brioche rolls.

Small Plates

Cheesy risotto cakes *with* herbed pistachio yoghurt

These scrumptious cakes don't take long because the rice is already cooked, and their shape makes them easier to heat all the way through than ball-shaped arancini. The quantities here are enough for two hungry people or four if you serve other dishes alongside. Just scale the ingredients up or down according to the amount of risotto you have left.

Leftovers: risotto, scraps of cheese, odds and ends of herbs

Makes 4 risotto cakes
Preparation: 30 minutes

For the herby yoghurt
20g (about 1 cup) mixed fresh herbs (leaves and fine stems), finely chopped
200g (1 cup) Greek yoghurt
20g (about 2 Tbsp) pistachios, toasted and roughly chopped
1 garlic clove, grated
2 Tbsp extra virgin olive oil
¼ tsp fine sea salt, or more to taste
A squeeze of lemon juice, to taste

For the risotto cakes
50g (6 Tbsp) plain (all-purpose) flour
60g (scant 1 cup) dried breadcrumbs
1 large egg
400g (about 3¼ cups) cold cooked risotto
25g (1oz) cheese that melts well (Cheddar, Gruyère, Emmental), chopped (avoid fresh mozzarella, as it's too wet)
Fine sea salt and freshly ground black pepper
Olive oil, for shallow frying

Stir all the herby yoghurt ingredients together and set aside.

For the risotto cakes, spread out the flour and the breadcrumbs on separate plates. Season the flour well with salt and pepper. Crack the egg into a shallow bowl and whisk with a fork.

Give the risotto a good stir to loosen it, then scoop a quarter of it into your hand. Press a quarter of the cheese into the centre and close the risotto around it, squeezing gently to seal. Flatten into a patty-shaped cake. Set aside and repeat with the remaining risotto and cheese.

Dip the cakes first into the flour, then the egg and then the breadcrumbs, coating them well. If the cakes are very soft, transfer to the fridge for 30 minutes (or 10 minutes in the freezer) to firm up for easier frying.

Set a heavy frying pan (skillet) over a high heat, then pour in enough oil to generously cover the base. Reduce the heat to medium and fry the cakes for 5–6 minutes on each side, or until golden and hot all the way through. Serve hot with the herby yoghurt alongside.

Smoky vegetable dip

This is a bit like babaganoush, the Middle Eastern aubergine (eggplant) dip, in that it's garlicky, smoky and moreish. I love broccoli in the mix but it's delicious with any veg – especially specimens that have, erm, 'caramelized' a bit too much in the oven.

Leftovers: cooked vegetables, herbs

Makes a small pot, but scale up the recipe if you have more leftover veg
Preparation: 15 minutes

125g (1 heaped cup) cooked vegetables (not mashed)
3 Tbsp Greek yoghurt
5 Tbsp extra virgin olive oil, plus extra to serve
1½ Tbsp tahini
2 Tbsp lemon juice, plus extra to taste
1 fat garlic clove
1 heaped tsp ground cumin
½ tsp smoked paprika, plus extra to taste
Fine sea salt and freshly ground black pepper
Chopped coriander (cilantro) or parsley, to serve

If your vegetables aren't already charred or crisp at the edges (after roasting, for example), griddle (grill) them in a hot pan to get some scorch marks.

Put the vegetables and all the remaining ingredients except the fresh herbs in a food processor. Pulse to a smoothish consistency, depending on how chunky or smooth you like your dip. (Alternatively, just chop finely by hand.) Taste and add more lemon juice or salt and pepper, or a splash of water if too thick.

Scrape into a bowl, drizzle with extra olive oil and sprinkle with the chopped herbs. Serve with warm flat bread for dipping.

Try ...
Making tortilla chips for scooping. Preheat the oven to 200°C/180°C fan/400°F/Gas mark 6. Brush both sides of some corn or flour tortilla wraps or flatbread with vegetable oil. Cut into triangles and arrange in a single layer on a baking sheet. Bake for about 6 minutes – keep an eye on them so they don't burn. They will crisp up as they cook. Sprinkle with salt before serving.

Using peanut butter or almond paste instead of tahini in the dip. You could also sprinkle the dip with chopped toasted walnuts or pistachios before serving.

Serving idea ...
Loosen with a bit more olive oil or a splash of water and serve as a sauce for meat or chicken.

Leftover soup muffins

This recipe is based on one I spotted in a French issue of *Elle* magazine. The idea sounds a bit crazy, but really does work. The soup serves as the liquid for the batter but also delivers lots of extra flavour. And it's a great way to use up bits of cheese.

Use any soup, but if it's chunky, blitz to a purée first in a blender or food processor. The amount of soup you need to add depends on how thick your soup is. Stir in just enough to make a thick batter that falls easily off the end of a spoon. If you have more leftover soup than specified in the recipe, just scale up the rest of the ingredients. Or freeze the soup for another time.

Leftovers: soup or stock, bits of cheese, odds and ends of herbs

Makes 4 large muffins
Preparation: 15 minutes
Cooking: 25 minutes

120g (scant 1 cup) plain (all-purpose) flour
1 tsp baking powder
1 tsp garlic powder/granules (optional)
¼ tsp fine sea salt
Freshly ground black pepper
2 Tbsp olive oil
1 large egg, lightly beaten
About 120ml (½ cup) leftover soup (more or less, as needed)
50g (about ½ cup) grated strong cheese (Cheddar, Comté, Gouda)
A small handful of fresh chopped herbs (optional)
1 spring onion (scallion), finely chopped (optional)

Preheat the oven to 180°C/160°C fan/350°F/Gas mark 4 and line 4 holes of a large muffin tray with paper cases or baking paper.

In a mixing bowl, whisk the flour, baking powder, garlic powder (if using) and salt and pepper together with a fork. Add the oil and egg to the flour mixture and stir. Then add enough of the soup to make a fairly thick batter. (See recipe introduction.)

Stir in the cheese and, if using, the herbs and spring onion. Add a splash more soup if the batter is too thick. Distribute between the muffin cases and bake for 25 minutes until golden. Delicious served warm.

Try ...
Adding a small handful of seeds – sunflower, nigella or poppy seeds work beautifully – to the batter with the cheese.

Whisking a teaspoonful of spice into the flour mixture such as cumin, paprika, curry powder or garam masala.

Other ideas ...
You can use leftover stock in the muffins. I've even used a wine and tomato braising liquid left over from slow cooking a shoulder of lamb, with excellent results.

Takeaway curry toastie *with* lime pickle

I used to wonder what to do with the curry left when, inevitably, we over-ordered takeaway. Would it be OK to eat the next day? Was it worth holding on to just a spoonful of sauce? Would anyone want repurposed curry anyway? The answer is a big delicious yes. It's hard to be precise about quantities because much depends on the size of your bread – just don't use too much filling or your toastie will leak. Make toasties with any leftover homemade stew or curry – it doesn't have to be takeaway. This is my favourite technique for making toasties, but if you're in possession of a proper toasted sandwich maker, use that.

Leftover: takeaway or homemade curry or stew, bits of cheese, naan or flatbread, curry sauce

Makes 1
Preparation: 10 minutes

Leftover meat, chicken or vegetable
    curry
Butter, for buttering the bread
2 medium slices of bloomer or
    sandwich loaf
Chopped coriander (cilantro) or
    parsley (optional)
35g (about ⅓ cup) grated Cheddar or
    other hard cheese (not Parmesan)
1 heaped tsp lime pickle (or
    other pickle)

Scoop the meat, chicken or veg out of the curry sauce and roughly chop.

Butter each slice of bread on one side and place buttered-side down on a chopping board. Spread one slice of bread with curry sauce and top with the chopped meat/chicken/veg, and herbs (if using). Top with cheese.

Spread the other slice of bread with pickle, then close the sandwich.

Heat a frying pan (skillet) over a medium heat and add the sandwich. Place a piece of baking paper on top, then a heavy object (I use a small pan with a can of beans – the weight compacts the filling, so the cheese melts more quickly).

Fry until golden underneath, then flip and repeat. Ensure the filling is piping hot before serving.

Try ...
Making naan bread pizzas: warm a splash of oil in an ovenproof frying pan and fry leftover naan bread, or any other flatbread, until golden underneath. Remove from the heat, spoon over some leftover curry sauce and top with grated cheese. Place under the grill (broiler) until the cheese is melted and bubbling.

Gooey chicken nuggets

I love croquetas, those fried bites with a cheese sauce filling, but can rarely be bothered to make them. That's why this quick and simple cheat's version – a cross between a nugget and a croqueta using cooked chicken – is so appealing. There is some shallow frying involved, but the rest is simple, and no bechamel sauce to make. Super moreish.

Leftovers: cooked chicken

Makes about 14
Preparation: 40 minutes

50g (6 Tbsp) plain (all-purpose) flour
100g (1¼ cups) dried breadcrumbs
1 large egg
Fine sea salt and freshly ground
    black pepper
Lemon wedges, to serve

For the nuggets

200g (7oz) cooked chicken, roughly
    chopped
240g (8½oz) grated pizza mozzarella
    (the ready-grated stuff, not fresh)
1 large egg
1 tsp cayenne pepper
1 tsp garlic granules
¼ tsp fine sea salt
Freshly ground black pepper
Vegetable oil, for shallow frying

For the dipping sauce
150g (¾ cup) Greek yoghurt
90g (scant ½ cup) mayonnaise
1 large garlic clove, grated
¼ tsp fine sea salt

Stir all the ingredients for the dipping sauce together and set aside.

Spread out the flour and breadcrumbs on separate plates. Season the flour with salt and pepper. Crack the egg into a shallow bowl and lightly beat with a fork.

Place all the nugget ingredients except the oil in the bowl of a food processor. Pulse until chunky and sticky – don't blitz to a paste. Roll the mixture into balls the size of large walnuts, then gently press into sausage shapes.

Pour enough oil into a small frying pan (skillet) to come 2cm (1in) up the sides and set it over a medium-high heat. The oil is hot enough for frying when a few breadcrumbs added to the pan immediately sizzle.

While the oil is heating, dip the nuggets first in the flour, then the egg and finally the breadcrumbs. Make sure they're well coated. Fry a few at a time for 5–6 minutes, turning now and then, until golden.

Transfer to a plate lined with paper towel. Serve hot, sprinkled with salt, lemon wedges for squeezing over, and the sauce alongside for dipping.

Try ...
Swapping Greek yoghurt for crème fraîche for the dipping sauce. Or add a teaspoonful of gochujang, harissa or other chilli paste to the yoghurt or crème fraiche to spice it up.

Cheeseboard puffs

There are few better uses for odds and ends of cheese than these golden orbs of gorgeousness – and perfect served with a glass of something cold. They take around 30 minutes from start to finish and will be gone in moments, they're that tasty. Use a mix of cheeses if you can, including soft ones like goat's or blue. Parmesan is particularly good sprinkled on top.

Leftovers: odds and ends of cheese

Makes about 20
Preparation: 10 minutes
Cooking: 20 minutes

60ml (4 Tbsp) full-fat (whole) milk
50g (3½ Tbsp) unsalted butter
½ tsp fine sea salt
60g (scant ½ cup) plain (all-purpose) flour
2 large eggs, lightly beaten
50g (about ½ cup) grated or crumbled cheese
A pinch of ground nutmeg
Freshly ground black pepper
Grated Parmesan, for sprinkling

Preheat the oven to 200°C/180°C fan/400°F/Gas mark 6 and line a baking sheet with baking paper.

Put the milk, butter, salt and 4 tablespoons water in a medium pan over a medium heat (don't use a small pan, as the mixture will splash up when you beat it). When the butter has melted, tip in the flour and stir vigorously with a wooden spoon to make a smooth stiff dough that comes away from the sides of the pan.

Take the pan off the heat and add the eggs bit by bit, beating well after each addition. Then, stir in the cheese, nutmeg and pepper.

Scoop spoonfuls of the mixture onto the prepared baking sheet – use two dessertspoons, one to scoop up the mixture, the other to slide it off the spoon. With a wet finger, smooth out any pointy bits of dough.

Sprinkle the tops with Parmesan and bake for 20 minutes, or until puffed and golden. Eat hot from the oven.

Try ...
Cutting the puffs in half horizontally and filling with curls of prosciutto and pickled veg.

Adding 25g (about ¼ cup) finely chopped toasted walnuts with the cheese.

Freezing the puffs. Arrange spoonfuls of the mixture on baking paper on a tray or chopping board that will fit inside your freezer. Transfer the uncooked puffs on the tray to the freezer. When frozen, transfer to a ziplock freezer bag (this process prevents them sticking together). Bake from frozen, as per the method.

Pasta fritters

I'm excessively fond of these fritters – they're crisp, tasty and score top marks for being speedy and easy. If using cooked pasta without sauce, add a small handful of chopped cooked vegetables to the mix (pasta-only fritters work fine, just add a bit more Parmesan). If you're repurposing cooked pasta with sauce – bolognaise, primavera, carbonara – make sure there's a good amount of pasta in the mix too, or the fritters might not hold together.

Leftovers: cold cooked pasta with or without sauce, cooked vegetables

Makes 4 fritters but easily scales up
Preparation: 15 minutes

150g (about 2 cups) cold leftover pasta
   (any shape), finely chopped
1 large egg
20g (¼ cup) grated Parmesan
A small handful of cooked veg,
   chopped small (optional)
1 small garlic clove, grated
½ Tbsp cornflour (cornstarch)
1 tsp pul biber (or 1 tsp smoked
   paprika plus a generous pinch
   of cayenne)
¼ tsp fine sea salt, plus extra for
   sprinkling
Olive oil, for shallow frying

Place all the ingredients except the olive oil in a mixing bowl and stir to combine everything.

Heat enough oil in a large frying pan (skillet) to cover the base generously. When hot, spoon in four equal mounds of the pasta mixture. Fry over a high heat for about 2 minutes until crisp underneath, then flip. Important: don't be tempted to flip sooner than this – the fritters need time to form a crust underneath, so they don't stick to the pan or fall apart. After the first minute of frying, press down gently on the fritter with an egg slice and push in stray bits of pasta. Fry for 1½ minutes on the other side.

Transfer to a plate lined with paper towel, sprinkle with salt and serve immediately.

Try ...
Leftover pasta, with or without sauce, in bubble and squeak, frittata and pies.

Roast dinner sausage rolls

When I was a schoolkid in Australia the warm smell of sausage rolls wafting under the classroom door heralded lunchtime. It meant my food order of choice – flaky buttery pastry wrapped around slightly greasy mystery meat – was on its way, borne warm in brown paper bags by lunch monitors.

The best thing about homemade sausage rolls is that you know what's in them. They're ideal to make after Thanksgiving dinner, Christmas lunch or a Sunday roast; turkey, ham, pigs in blankets, lamb, beef, chicken, roasties and vegetables can all be wrapped in pastry with brilliant results.

Leftovers: cooked meat and vegetables, vegetarian sausages or meat alternatives

Makes 16
Preparation: 25 minutes plus
*   15 minutes cooling*
Cooking: about 25 minutes

2 Tbsp olive oil
1 onion, finely chopped
1 plump garlic clove, finely chopped
1 tsp dried mixed herbs
450g (1lb) leftover cooked meat and/or
    vegetables
2 tsp chipotle paste or other chilli
    paste
2 tsp crème fraîche, cream or milk
    (if needed)
40g (3 Tbsp) cold butter
1 sheet ready-rolled puff pastry, about
    35 x 23cm (14 x 9in) or roughly 330g
    (11½oz) from a block
1 egg, lightly beaten
½ tsp nigella seeds
Fine sea salt and freshly ground
    black pepper

Preheat the oven to 220°C/200°C fan/425°F/Gas mark 7 and line a baking sheet with baking paper.

Warm the olive oil in a large frying pan (skillet) and gently fry the onion with a pinch of salt over a medium heat until soft and translucent, about 10 minutes. Add the garlic and mixed herbs and fry for a couple more minutes. Transfer to a large mixing bowl and leave to cool to room temperature.

Chop the leftovers by hand or pulse in a food processor. Don't overdo it; the mixture should be rough not smooth. Season generously with salt and pepper.

Transfer the leftovers to the bowl with the onions and add the chipotle paste and crème fraîche. Grate in the butter. Mix well.

Lay the pastry sheet on a lightly floured work surface with a short side closest to you. Fold the top edge down to meet the lower edge and lightly press to make a crease along the centre. Unfold and cut along the crease to make two smaller rectangles.

Fold each of the small rectangles in half along the short side. Unfold and cut along the crease to make four rectangles 9 x 23cm (3½ x 9in). Place a quarter of the filling along a long side of each pastry rectangle. Squeeze the filling as you go so it holds together. Brush the facing long edge with egg, then firmly roll into a log. Press to seal firmly. Repeat with the remaining filling and pastry.

Cut each log into four equal pieces and transfer to the prepared baking sheet. Brush with egg and sprinkle with nigella seeds. Bake for 25 minutes or until puffed and golden. Serve hot.

Try ...
Adding a small quantity of cooked lentils, rice or other grains to the filling if you need to stretch out your leftovers.

If you have uncooked sausages to use up – they're among the most wasted foods – sausage rolls are the answer. Heat a splash of olive oil in a large frying pan (skillet) and gently fry 1 tsp of fennel seeds for a minute or so, then add a finely chopped onion. Fry gently for 10 minutes. Remove the pan from the heat and add the meat from 450g (1lb) sausages (just snip the casing and squeeze it out), some chopped fresh herbs and lots of salt and pepper. Mix well and leave to cool. Fill the pastry and bake according to the method above.

Light Meals

Lettuce, herb *and* pea soup *with* goat's cheese *and* nigella seeds

Lettuce is one of the most wasted foods – whole ones as well as bagged salad. But even when wilted and past its best – or you just don't fancy eating any more salad – there are gorgeous ways to use it up. This soup is one of them. I've made it with all sorts of less-than-perky (but definitely not slimy) leaves and herbs, including a whole batch made with rocket (arugula). Serve warm, with goat's cheese squished on toast. Or try it chilled on a hot day.

Double up this recipe if you have lots of leaves and herbs to use up. It keeps well in the fridge for a day or so.

Leftovers: lettuce, rocket, fresh herbs

Serves 2
Preparation: 35 minutes

200g (7oz) salad leaves (lettuce, rocket/arugula, mixed leaves), plus extra to serve
A handful of soft fresh herbs (leaves and thin stalks), plus extra to serve
2 Tbsp olive oil
1 onion, chopped
1 garlic clove, chopped
1 medium potato, peeled and cut into very small dice
500ml (17fl oz) hot chicken or vegetable stock
100g (about ¾ cup) frozen peas
A squeeze of lemon juice
Fine sea salt

To serve
Nigella seeds
Soft goat's cheese, crumbled
2 radishes, finely sliced (optional)

Bring a large pan of salted water to the boil. Meanwhile, have a large bowl of cold water standing by. Add the salad leaves and herbs to the boiling water and blanch for 20 seconds. Drain and add to the iced water, then drain again and set aside.

Warm the olive oil in a large pan and fry the onion with a pinch of salt until soft and translucent, about 8 minutes. Add the garlic and potato and cook until tender, adding a splash of water if anything starts to stick.

Add the stock to the pan and bring to a gentle simmer, scraping up any bits that have stuck to the bottom. Add the peas and simmer until just tender. Add the blanched lettuce and herbs, pushing them under the stock. Cook for a couple of minutes, then take the pan off the heat. Pour the soup into a colander (strainer) and collect the liquid in a jug underneath. Transfer the leaves and veg to a blender and add a generous splash of the stock. Blitz until smooth. Add more stock bit by bit, blitzing between additions, to produce the soup consistency you love. Add a good squeeze of lemon juice; taste and add more salt if needed.

If serving the soup cold, chill until needed. If serving warm, return it to the pan and warm through. Place a few salad and herb leaves in two bowls and pour the soup over. Sprinkle with nigella seeds and crumbled goat's cheese and adorn with the radishes (if using).

Try ...
Adding a spoonful or two of cooked butter (lima) beans or chickpeas (garbanzo beans) as 'croutons' at the end if you have some to use up. If you have time, fry these first in olive oil with a good pinch of paprika to crisp up a little.

Using leeks, spring onions (scallions) or fennel instead of onion as the base for the soup.

Adding wild garlic (ramps) to your assemblage of leaves for a more intense flavour.

Bread tart *with* greens, pine nuts *and* raisins

Here's a beautiful way to use up surplus bread and vegetables. It's miraculous how bread can be repurposed in such an elegant way. I've made this tart case with white bread, sourdough and a sliced seedy loaf – both stale and fresh – and they all work well. The type and freshness of your bread will dictate how much water you need, so add it gradually. You can top the tart with leftovers other than greens, too, such as roast squash/pumpkin, sweet (bell) pepper, red onion and root vegetables, or griddled/fried mushrooms, asparagus or courgettes.

Leftovers: stale bread, lettuce, leafy greens, cooked vegetables

Serves 4–6
Preparation: 25 minutes
Cooking: 45 minutes

For the tart case
Olive oil, for oiling
150g (5½oz) leftover bread, including crusts, torn into pieces
1 large egg
40g (½ cup) grated Parmesan
½ tsp dried mixed herbs
Plain (all-purpose) flour, for dusting

For the filling
115g (½ cup) cream cheese
40g (½ cup) grated Parmesan
1 Tbsp double (heavy) cream, or more as needed
Finely grated zest of ½ lemon
Fine sea salt and ground black pepper

For the greens
2 Tbsp pine nuts
1 Tbsp olive oil
2 Tbsp butter, plus extra if needed
200g (7oz) cooked and uncooked greens: finely sliced kale, spring onions (scallions) chopped into 3cm (1¼in) pieces, sliced chard, baby spinach leaves, lettuce, sliced Brussels sprouts or cabbage
A large handful of fresh herbs such as parsley, basil, tarragon
30g (about 3 Tbsp) sultanas (golden raisins)

Preheat the oven to 180°C/160°C fan/350°F/Gas mark 4 and place a baking sheet inside. Liberally brush a 23cm (9in) loose-bottomed tart tin with oil. (The tart will be tricky to remove if the tin isn't thoroughly coated, including fluted edges, so be generous.)

For the tart case, put the bread, egg, Parmesan and herbs in the bowl of a food processor. Blitz to a smoothish sticky dough, gradually adding 1–2 tablespoons water (or more if needed). Scoop the dough onto a well-floured work surface and briefly knead with lightly floured hands. Shape into a disc. Re-flour your hands and place the disc in the centre of the oiled tart tin. Working from the centre, press the dough outwards so it fills the base of the tin evenly. Press into the edges to make a slight ridge – it doesn't need to go all the way up the sides.

Bake for 25 minutes or until the edges have browned a little and the middle is dry – watch that it doesn't burn. Transfer the tart case, still in its tin, to a wire rack to cool.

Meanwhile, beat together all the filling ingredients and set aside.

For the greens, toast the pine nuts until golden in a large dry frying pan (skillet). Scoop into a bowl.

Return the pan to the heat, and add the oil and butter. When melted, add tougher uncooked greens like kale and spring onions (scallions). Fry for 3–4 minutes until almost tender. Add softer greens next and the sultanas (golden raisins). Fry over a medium heat until all the greens are soft. Stir in the pine nuts, any cooked greens and herbs. Taste and adjust the seasoning if needed. Set aside for 10 minutes to cool.

Spoon the creamy filling into the tart case and spread to cover the base evenly. Top with the cooked greens. Slide the tart back onto the baking sheet in the oven and bake for 20 minutes or until the tops of the vegetables are slightly charred. Loosen the edges of the tart case with a knife before releasing from the tin. Serve warm.

Gooey chip tortilla

The technique for making this glorious tortilla – golden on the outside, custardy in the middle – is inspired by the celebrated version served at Bar Nestor in the Spanish coastal resort of San Sebastián. But instead of frying potatoes for the purpose, mine uses leftover chips (our chippy always serves so many with fish suppers we never finish them). It works a treat. It's heavy on olive oil but this isn't a time for skimping.

Leftovers: potato chips

Makes/serves 4–6
Preparation: 1 hour

90ml (6 Tbsp) olive oil
2 onions, halved and finely sliced
3 garlic cloves, finely chopped
6 large eggs
300g (10½oz) cooked chips (French fries), roughly chopped
Fine sea salt (if needed) and freshly ground black pepper

Warm 4 tablespoons of the olive oil in a 23cm (9in) frying pan (skillet). Add the onions and a generous pinch of salt. Fry very gently over a medium-low heat for 35 minutes, stirring regularly, until soft and translucent. Add the garlic and fry for 5 minutes more. Set aside.

In a large mixing bowl, beat the eggs using a fork. Add the onions, chips (French fries), 1 teaspooon of salt (or just a pinch if your chips already taste salty) and some black pepper.

Wash and dry the onion pan and set it over a high heat. Add the remaining 2 tablespoons oil and use a pastry brush to brush it up the sides so the whole pan is well coated. When the pan is very hot, pour in the egg and chip mixture. Immediately reduce the heat to medium-low. Spread out the mixture evenly, poking under any chips that are sticking up. Cook for 8 minutes or until a 1-cm (½-in) wide rim forms around the edge that is cooked, puffed and firm, while the centre is still wet.

Place a rimless baking sheet or flat plate over the pan and quickly invert the tortilla. Carefully lift off the pan, return the pan to the heat, then slide the tortilla back into the pan. The cooked side will be facing upwards.

Using a spatula, tuck the edges of the tortilla in and under so it regains its curved edges and slightly domed shape. Cook for a further 3 minutes over a medium-low heat.

Slide the tortilla onto a plate or board and serve warm.

Try ...
Reheating leftover chips in the microwave, then stuffing them between thick slices of white buttered bread. Add ketchup, brown sauce, mayonnaise or vinegar.

Using leftover chips in bubble and squeak or hash (see page 31) or in pies.

Braised greens *with* melted sardines on toast

A hotchpotch of leafy greens – either cooked or retrieved from the depths of the salad crisper drawer – is dragged around a hot pan with olive oil, garlic and cooked-down sardines to make a brilliant and adaptable light lunch. If you're using cooked greens, or uncooked tender leaves like baby spinach or lettuce, don't bother blanching them first.

Leftovers: cooked and uncooked leafy greens including lettuce; other cooked vegetables

Serves 2
Preparation: 25 minutes

150g–200g (5½–7oz) uncooked leafy greens such as cabbage, kale, Little Gem (Boston lettuce) or chard, sliced, or about 140g (5oz) cooked greens, squeezed of excess moisture
1 x 120g (4¼oz) can sardines in olive oil
6 cherry tomatoes, halved
1 garlic clove, finely sliced
A good pinch of chilli flakes
A squeeze of lemon juice, plus a lemon wedge to serve
Fine sea salt and freshly ground black pepper
Toast, to serve

Blanch uncooked greens in boiling salted water for 3 minutes. Drain well and set aside.

Set a small frying pan (skillet) over a medium heat and warm the oil from the can of sardines. Add the tomatoes and fry until slightly charred and starting to collapse. Add the garlic and fry for another 2 minutes. Add the sardines to the pan and break them up with the side of a spoon. Turn them over in the oil to coat, then fry until they start to disintegrate.

Stir the cooked greens into the sardines and tomatoes and fry for a few minutes to warm through.

Sprinkle over the chilli flakes and lemon juice then season with salt and lots of black pepper. Serve on hot toast with a lemon wedge for squeezing.

Try ...
Replacing some of the greens with other leftover cooked vegetables: sliced courgettes (zucchini) and red sweet (bell) peppers work beautifully.

Sprinkling over chopped capers at the end as a foil to the richness of the sardines.

Using other kinds of canned fish. Mackerel or pilchards are delicious, and sardines in tomato sauce are good, too.

Adding a couple of finely chopped anchovy fillets to the oil with the tomatoes.

Egg in a nest

My mother-in-law used to make this sweet little dish for my husband when he was a child (I think a hamburger patty was involved as well). It's a plain, simple and delicious way to use up leftover mashed potato – great for kids or as a light lunch served with salad or vegetables on the side. An asparagus spear poked into the yolk would be a fine thing, too. Note: don't use cheese other than Parmesan in the mash, otherwise the potato will melt into a puddle.

Leftovers: mashed potato

Serves 1
Preparation: about 5 minutes
Cooking: about 15–20 minutes

150g (about ¾ cup) cold mashed potato
10g (about 2 Tbsp) grated Parmesan
A small handful of finely sliced
  greens, spring onion (scallion)
  or fresh herbs
A pinch of ground nutmeg
A splash of milk, if needed
1 egg
Fine sea salt and freshly ground
  black pepper

Preheat the oven to 200°C/180°C fan/400°F/Gas mark 6 and line a baking sheet with baking paper.

Mix together the mashed potato, Parmesan, greens/herbs and nutmeg. Season with salt and pepper. Loosen with a little milk if necessary to achieve a smooth and creamy consistency that is stiff but not dry and crumbly (it needs to hold its shape in the oven).

Spoon the potato onto the prepared baking sheet, shaping it into a round mound about 4cm (1½in) high. Create a deep indent in the middle, large enough to hold an egg (but don't crack it in yet!). Leave a thin layer of potato at the bottom of the indent.

Bake for 10–15 minutes or until lightly golden in places. Remove from the oven and crack the egg into the indent. Sprinkle with a little Parmesan and bake for a further 4–6 minutes, or until the whites are just set. Watch it carefully, as the egg will overcook in the blink of an eye.

Try ...
Flavouring the mash with a generous pinch of garlic granules, paprika, cayenne pepper or garam masala.

Adding other vegetables to the mix – mashed carrot, squash, parsnip, celeriac (celery root) – but make sure at least half of it is potato.

Anything goes brown butter frittata

This is a tasty vehicle for all manner of leftovers. Throw in cooked veg or uncooked odds and ends from the salad crisper drawer (cook these first, except leafy greens, which just need finely slicing). Those annoying scoops of pasta left in the pot can go in too, with sauce or without, as well as leftover cooked rice and grains, and oddments of cheese. Parked with brown-butter-scented eggs and cream, those remnants taste magical.

Leftovers: odds and ends of cooked or uncooked vegetables, cooked pasta/rice/grains, cheese, meat, firm tofu, the end of a pot of cream, soured cream or crème fraîche

Serves 2–4
Preparation: 15 minutes
Cooking: 12 minutes

About 1 densely packed coffee mug of mixed leftovers
3 Tbsp butter
1 small onion, finely chopped
5 large eggs
60g (¼ cup) cream, soured cream or crème fraîche
40g (about ½ cup) grated cheese, ideally including Parmesan
Fine sea salt

Preheat the oven to 180°C/160°C fan/350°F/Gas mark 4 and tip the leftovers into a mixing bowl. Set aside.

Set a 20cm (8in) ovenproof frying pan (skillet) over a high heat and add the butter. Cook, swirling the pan, until dark brown and smelling nutty. Pour into a small heatproof bowl, scraping in any caramelized bits, too. Return the pan to a medium heat. Add back in a tablespoon of the brown butter and the onion. Gently fry with a pinch of salt until very soft, about 8 minutes. Take off the heat and transfer to the mixing bowl with the leftovers.

Whisk together the eggs, cream, grated cheese, another tablespoon of the brown butter and a generous pinch of salt. Add to the bowl with the leftovers and stir to combine.

Wipe out the pan and set over a high heat. Add the remaining brown butter and when very hot, pour in the egg and leftovers. Briefly stir with a silicone spatula then shake the pan so the mixture settles evenly, and the leftovers are mostly covered by egg.

Cook for 1 minute undisturbed, or until the edge is starting to set. Transfer to the oven immediately and cook for 12 minutes, or until the middle is barely set. Serve hot or cold.

Try ...
Topping with more grated or crumbled cheese (feta and halloumi are lovely) before sliding the frittata into the oven.

Arranging very finely sliced uncooked courgettes (zucchini), mushrooms and/or tomatoes on top before going into the oven.

What about ...
Stuffing slices of frittata into soft buttered bread rolls with lettuce leaves and a thick slick of mayonnaise.

Beef *and* blue cheese pizzette *with* garlic butter

These splendid mini pizzas topped with roast beef and blue cheese are a breeze to make and ridiculously easy to put away. I adore the deeply savoury punch of the classic beef-and-blue pairing, but go for a milder cheese if that's what you have. If you have more leftovers to use, just scale up the recipe.

Leftovers: roast beef, scraps of blue cheese

Makes four 12cm (4½in) pizzette
Preparation: 20 minutes
Cooking: 18 minutes

For the dough
120g (scant 1 cup) self-raising (self-rising) flour, plus extra for dusting
1 tsp baking powder
120g (scant ¾ cup) Greek yoghurt
1 tsp vegetable oil
½ tsp fine sea salt

For the garlic butter
1 Tbsp butter
1 garlic clove, crushed

For the topping
170g (6oz) roast beef, chopped
80g (2¾oz) blue cheese, crumbled or chopped
Fresh parsley, roughly chopped

Preheat the oven to 220°C/200°C fan/425°F/Gas mark 7 and line a baking sheet with baking paper. Put all the ingredients for the dough in a mixing bowl and mix with your hands until combined. Turn out onto a floured work surface and knead lightly to bring the dough together – it will be sticky, so dust over a little flour when needed. Roll into four equal balls and set aside.

Meanwhile, for the garlic butter, melt the butter in a small pan. Add the garlic and cook gently for 1 minute or so, then move the pan to sit half-on a very low heat.

Use your fingertips to lightly press the dough balls out into 12cm (4½in) discs. Arrange on the prepared baking sheet and brush all over with the garlic butter. Divide the beef equally between the pizzette and top with the cheese. Bake for 18 minutes or until the bases are golden and the cheese bubbling. Sprinkle with fresh parsley and serve immediately.

Try ...
Exploring the infinite possibilities for piling leftover meat and cheese onto these tasty discs: lamb and feta or Emmental; ham and Gruyère; shredded chicken and sliced Brie or Camembert; sausages and a sharp Cheddar.

Crispy chilli rice *with* fried egg *and* greens

Fried rice is delicious but crispy rice is an even better way to deploy cold leftovers. It's made by scorching rice in a hot pan until the grains turn crunchy and deeply tasty. In many cuisines, crispy rice is treasured; it features in the Persian dish tahdig, for example, and Spanish paella (where the prized crispy bits at the bottom of the pan command their own name – socarrat). Here, I've spiked cold rice with chilli sauce and tomato purée (paste), and then seared it in a thin layer. The recipe serves two but for more than this, fry the rice in batches. If there is too much in the pan it will steam rather than crisp up.

Leftovers: rice

Serves 2
Preparation: 15 minutes

For the rice
260g (generous 2 cups) cold cooked rice
3–4 Tbsp sriracha sauce or chilli crisp oil (depending on how spicy you want your rice)
1½ Tbsp soy sauce
2 Tbsp tomato purée (paste)
2 tsp sesame oil, plus extra for drizzling
2 Tbsp vegetable oil, for frying
1 spring onion (scallion), finely sliced

Fried eggs, to serve
Steamed greens, such as pak choi (bok choy), to serve

Mix together in a bowl all the rice ingredients except the vegetable oil and spring onion (scallion). Make sure all the rice grains are well coated.

Heat a large heavy frying pan (skillet), non-stick ideally, until very hot. Add the vegetable oil and swirl to cover the base.

Add the rice, spread it out over the base of the pan in a thin layer and flatten with a spatula. Fry over a medium-high heat for 2 minutes without disturbing. Drizzle a little sesame oil over the rice and flip chunks of it over – it should be burnished and crisp in parts. Fry for another 2 minutes, pressing down again with the spatula.

Flip the rice again. It should be a mixture of crisp and not so crisp grains. If this hasn't happened yet, keep frying, flipping and pressing but be careful not to overcook the rice – you don't want it dry and hard. Serve the rice hot, with a fried egg, greens and spring onion sprinkled on top.

Roast beef *with* tomatoes, walnuts *and* tonnato sauce

I drape this dreamy creamy Italian sauce on everything from eggs and vegetables to salads and chicken – and a slick is pretty good in sandwiches too. Tonnato really shines paired with red meat – veal, as it's traditionally served with in Piedmont, but also with cold slices of leftover roast beef, as I suggest here. This recipe will make a bit more sauce than you need for the quantity of beef I've specified but I'll hazard a guess you'll use it all. It's strangely versatile for a sauce made with fish.

Leftovers: roast beef, chicken or lamb

Serves 2–4
Preparation: 15 minutes

250g (9oz) sliced cold roast beef
100g (3½oz) tomatoes, sliced
A small handful of parsley, finely chopped
25g (about ¼ cup) walnuts, toasted and roughly chopped

For the tonnato sauce
70g (2½oz) canned tuna in oil, drained
2 anchovy fillets in oil, drained
1 Tbsp capers (rinsed well if salted)
1 large egg yolk
1 large garlic clove
1 tsp white wine vinegar, plus extra to taste
3 Tbsp olive oil
3 Tbsp vegetable oil
Fine sea salt and freshly ground white pepper (or black pepper is fine)

Put all the sauce ingredients except the olive oil and groundnut oil in a small bowl or jug if you're using an immersion blender, or in a food processor or blender. Blitz to a paste. Gradually trickle both the oils, blitzing constantly, to make a thick sauce. Add salt, pepper and more vinegar to taste.

Spread a thin layer of the sauce over a serving platter, then arrange the roast beef and tomatoes on top. Drizzle over more of the sauce and scatter the parsley and walnuts on top.

Tip
Use the egg white for the buckwheat crunch recipe on page 152.

Takeaway curry noodle soup

This is another excellent way to squeeze every last drop out of a curry, whether takeaway or homemade. A good amount of sauce is key to make this really tasty – in fact, it's excellent even if you only have sauce left. For other ideas on how to use up leftover curry see the curry toastie on page 52 or the tips and tricks on page 180.

Leftovers: curry or stew, fresh herbs, rice

Serves 2
Preparation: 20 minutes

1 serving of your favourite noodles
A splash of sesame oil
About 250g (9oz) leftover curry and sauce
250ml (1 cup plus 2 tsp) chicken or vegetable stock

Optional add-ins:
Cooked green vegetables or finely sliced (uncooked) leafy greens like lettuce, pak choi (bok choy) or baby spinach
A splash of cream or coconut milk (not needed for a coconut-based curry)
A spoonful or two of cooked grains, or rice

To serve
Chopped fresh herbs, such as coriander (cilantro) or parsley
Lime juice
Chilli crisp or chilli oil
Hard-boiled egg, halved (optional)

Cook the noodles according to the packet instructions. Drain, toss with a little sesame oil and set aside.

Scoop any meat, chicken, vegetables and/or tofu out of the curry, leaving just the sauce behind. Chop any large pieces into bite-sized chunks.

Pour the curry sauce and stock into a pan and heat gently, stirring. Add the chopped meat/chicken/veg/tofu and the noodles. If the soup needs bulking out, toss in some finely sliced greens, cooked vegetables or grains, and simmer gently until everything is warmed through. Add a splash of cream or coconut milk if you fancy.

Serve sprinkled with the herbs, a squeeze of lime juice, a splash of chilli crisp or chilli oil and boiled egg (if using).

Refreshing tomato, almond *and* mint soup

Overripe tomatoes and stale bread come together in blissful union in this intensely flavourful and cooling soup, which is my version of pappa al pomodoro, the classic Italian cold soup. Put aside any prejudice you might have against soup that isn't served hot – this is hard to beat on a summer's day when the temperature makes cooking unappealing. It's also very simple to pull together, especially if you're giving it to guests, as it's best made in advance and served chilled.

Leftovers: overripe tomatoes, stale bread

Serves 4
Preparation: 5 minutes plus at least 2 hours chilling time

750g (1lb 10oz) ripe tomatoes, chopped
75g (2½oz) stale bread, torn
40g (⅓ cup) blanched almonds
3 garlic cloves, chopped
3 Tbsp extra virgin olive oil, plus extra for drizzling
½ tsp fine sea salt, or to taste
3 large mint leaves, plus finely sliced leaves to serve
Thinly sliced ham, chopped small or shredded, to serve (optional)

Put the tomatoes, bread, almonds, garlic, oil, salt and mint in a blender and blitz until completely smooth. Push the mixture through a sieve set over a bowl, pressing down on any solids to extract as much liquid as possible.

Return the liquid to the blender (discarding any solids) and add a splash of water if too thick. Blitz again. Taste and add more salt or mint if needed (there should be just a hint of the latter).

Chill, ideally at least for a couple of hours. Serve topped with finely sliced mint and ham (if using) and a drizzle of extra virgin olive oil.

Griddled pear *and* bitter leaf salad *with* almonds *and* elderflower dressing

Pears can be gems of the fruit bowl if you catch them at the right moment, but often they stubbornly refuse to ripen and taste disappointing. The solution is to fry them to tenderness, as I've done in this beautiful salad. Their sweetness marries beautifully with the bitter leaves, salty cheese or ham, and almonds. The perfumed dressing unites the flavours of this simple and pretty salad.

Leftovers: unripe or hard pears

Serves 2 generously as a starter
Preparation: 15 minutes

1 Tbsp olive oil
20g (scant ¼ cup) blanched almonds
80g (2¾oz) red or white chicory leaves, separated
4 Brussels sprouts, outer green leaves separated, inner core finely sliced
3 radishes, finely sliced
1 large or 2 small firm or underripe pears
Lemon juice, for sprinkling
15g (½oz) Parmesan or pecorino, shaved, or 3 slices of prosciutto
Fine sea salt and freshly ground black pepper

For the dressing
3 Tbsp elderflower cordial (or 1 tsp of apricot jam or floral honey)
3 Tbsp cider vinegar
80ml (¼ cup plus 2 Tbsp) vegetable oil
Fine sea salt and freshly ground black pepper

Put the dressing ingredients in a lidded jar, seal and shake to combine. Set aside.

Warm the olive oil in a frying pan (skillet) over a medium heat and fry the almonds until golden. Scoop out and set aside. Take the pan off the heat but don't wash it yet.

Place the chicory, sprouts, radishes and half the almonds in a large bowl.

Peel, core and quarter the pear(s) or, if large, halve each quarter. Transfer to a bowl as you go and squeeze over a little lemon juice to prevent browning. Season with salt.

Reheat the remaining oil in the pan and fry the pears until lightly golden on all sides. Take the pan off the heat.

Toss the bitter leaves with 3–4 tablespoons of the dressing – enough to coat everything well. Place on a serving platter or individual plates, scatter over the remaining almonds and drizzle with more dressing (you might not need it all). Top with the cheese or prosciutto and serve immediately.

Try ...
Using 4 generous spoonfuls of strong soft cheese like taleggio, gorgonzola or dolcelatte instead of Parmesan or pecorino.

No pears? Halve and destone apricots, peaches or plums and fry in the same way.

Indian-spiced veg bowl *with* crispy chickpeas *and* chutney dressing

This tasty bowlful is inspired by a dish I enjoyed at Lulu, Alice Waters' bistro in Los Angeles. It's my favourite kind of flexible and doable salad: little bits of this and that retrieved from the fridge and store cupboard (pantry), elevated and brought together with a vibrant dressing. Think of this as a template and adapt according to the ingredients you need to use up. That bendy stick of celery finally has a home...

Leftovers: odds and ends of cooked and uncooked vegetables

Serves 2 generously
Preparation: 15 minutes
Cooking: 6½ minutes

1 x 400g (14oz) can chickpeas
  (garbanzo beans)
2 eggs
3 Tbsp vegetable oil
2 tsp curry powder or garam masala
A handful of cooked and/or finely
  sliced raw veg: roast cauliflower,
  sweet potatoes, raw mushrooms,
  cucumber, celery or pepper
A handful of sliced green leaves: baby
  spinach, lettuce or fresh herbs
4 radishes, finely sliced
1 Tbsp chopped raisins or sultanas
  (golden raisins), optional
Coriander (cilantro) leaves
2 lime wedges, to serve

For the green chutney dressing
15g (½oz) mint leaves
60g (2¼oz) coriander (cilantro)
1½ Tbsp unsweetened desiccated
  (dried, shredded) coconut
½ tsp ground cumin
2 Tbsp lemon juice, plus extra if needed
1 plump garlic clove
1 small green chilli
1 heaped tsp chopped ginger
1 Tbsp vegetable oil
Fine sea salt

Drain the chickpeas (garbanzo beans), reserving the liquid (see page 162 for how to use it in a chocolate mousse). Rinse with cold water, then drain again. Rub dry with a clean tea towel (dish towel), then spread out on paper towel.

Bring a pan of water to the boil and lower in the eggs. Boil for 6½ minutes, drain and run under cold water. Peel and set aside.

Meanwhile, put all the chutney dressing ingredients in a blender and blitz, adding enough cold water for a smooth sauce the consistency of single (light) cream. Taste and add more lemon juice or salt if needed. Set aside.

Warm the vegetable oil in a large frying pan (skillet) and add the chickpeas. Sprinkle over the curry powder and turn to coat in the oil. Fry over a medium-high heat, shaking the pan frequently, until the chickpeas begin to darken and crisp up a little. Take the pan off the heat and toss the chickpeas with one-third of the dressing.

Distribute the chickpeas, vegetables, leaves and radishes between two bowls and drizzle over more dressing. Top with the eggs (halved), radishes, raisins (if using) and coriander (cilantro). Serve with the lime wedges.

Variations ...
There are infinite ways to incorporate leftovers into this bowl. Check if you have any unfinished packets of nuts, seeds, grains or dried fruit. Frozen peas are a great addition: place a couple of spoonfuls in a mug, cover with freshly boiled water, and leave to stand for 5 minutes. Chopped fresh fruit would be good too.

Try ...
Sprinkling sliced mushrooms, if you're using them in this salad, with lemon juice and salt for bags of extra flavour. Leave to marinate while you prepare the rest of the salad and then add with the vegetables.

Curried potato pancakes *with* smoked fish *and* mango chutney crème fraîche

If you've ever looked at a scoop of mashed potato left in the pot and wondered if it's worth keeping, this recipe is for you. Or rather, it's for everyone, because we've all thrown small amounts of mash away. This is a real favourite in my household and a great example of how a delicious meal can be framed around a small quantity of humble leftovers.

Leftovers: mashed potatoes

Serves 2 generously
Preparation: 40 minutes

For the mango chutney crème fraîche
100g (scant ½ cup) full-fat crème fraîche or soured cream
2 tsp mango chutney
2 Tbsp chopped coriander (cilantro), plus extra leaves to serve
A squeeze of lemon juice
Fine sea salt and freshly ground black pepper
140g (5oz) smoked mackerel fillets

For the pancakes
200g (about 1 cup) mashed potato
Up to 75ml (5 Tbsp) full-fat (whole) milk
40g (generous ¼ cup) plain (all-purpose) flour
½ tsp baking powder
1 tsp medium curry powder
¼ tsp fine sea salt
1 large egg
1 Tbsp vegetable oil, or more if needed

Coriander (cilantro) leaves, to serve
Lemon juice, to serve

Stir all the ingredients for the mango chutney crème fraiche except the mackerel together in a medium bowl. Flake in the mackerel, mix gently and set aside.

Put the mashed potato into a mixing bowl. Stir in enough milk to loosen to a creamy consistency. Add the flour, baking powder, curry powder and salt and stir well. Beat in the egg and then more milk as needed to make a smooth, thick batter.

Heat a large heavy frying pan (skillet) over a medium-high heat. Add the oil and swirl to coat. Add large spoonfuls of batter to the pan to make four 9–10cm (about 4in) pancakes.

Cook for 2 minutes, or until golden underneath. Flip and cook for 1 minute more or until cooked through, then remove from the heat.

Serve the pancakes topped with the mango chutney crème fraîche, coriander (cilantro) leaves and a squeeze of lemon juice.

Try...
Reheating cold mashed potato with leftover gravy and/or dripping from the roasting tray for a gorgeous side.

Griddled Little Gem *with* anchovy hollandaise

If there's a better way to use up egg yolks, I'm yet to discover it. And this luscious sauce, one of my absolute favourites, takes no time, especially if you use a blender. I've specified Little Gem (Boston lettuce) but any lettuce with a firm heart, like Cos (Romaine) or even Iceberg, works beautifully – just cut them into wedges. A poached or fried egg served alongside would be perfectly in order.

Leftovers: egg yolks, lettuce

Serves 2–4
Preparation: 20 minutes

2 large or 4 medium Little Gem
    (Boston lettuce), halved or quartered
    lengthways, depending on size
Olive oil, for brushing
Pecorino or Parmesan, grated, for
    sprinkling

For the hollandaise
3 large egg yolks
1 Tbsp cider vinegar, or more to taste
3 anchovy fillets in oil, drained and
    roughly chopped
1 large garlic clove, grated
Fine sea salt (if needed)
A pinch of cayenne pepper
120g (½ cup) unsalted butter, cut into
    small pieces

Start with the hollandaise. If using an immersion blender, put all the ingredients except the butter in a small bowl or jug. Otherwise add to a standard blender, or a mixing bowl if whisking by hand. Blitz or whisk until creamy. Set aside.

Melt the butter in a small pan. While it's still hot, trickle it slowly into the egg mixture, blitzing or beating constantly, to produce a creamy, thick sauce. Taste and add more salt, vinegar or cayenne if needed. Working quickly (you want to serve the sauce while it's warm), heat a large griddle (grill pan) or frying pan (skillet) over a high heat. Brush the lettuce pieces with oil. Griddle/fry until charred in patches and tender on the outside but still retaining some bite in the middle.

Serve immediately, with the hollandaise spooned over and showered with grated cheese.

Try ...
Using endive or slender cabbage wedges instead of lettuce. Once charred on the outside, reduce the heat to low and cook until tender in the middle.

What about ...
Pouring the hollandaise over roast vegetables, leftover roast meat, chicken and fish. It's also terrific used as a condiment in sandwiches stuffed with leftovers.

Ham *and* sauerkraut croque

Based on the classic croque monsieur (the fancy French ham and cheese toastie), this one uses a thick slice of good bread instead of the traditional two slices of fluffy white. I've introduced sauerkraut because I love the flavour thwack it adds to the rich cheese and salty ham combo. It's perfect for using up post-Christmas or Thanksgiving ham but shredded turkey (or chicken) would be great too, mind you.

Leftovers: ham, odds and ends of cheese

Serves 2 generously
Preparation: about 30 minutes

20g (1½ Tbsp) butter, plus extra
    for spreading
1 garlic clove, peeled and bruised
    with the side of a knife
20g (2 Tbsp plus 1 tsp) plain
    (all-purpose) flour
200ml (generous ¾ cup) full-fat
    (whole) milk
1 Tbsp white wine
¼ tsp Dijon mustard
A pinch of ground nutmeg
80g (about ¾ cup) grated strong
    cheese – Cheddar, Gruyère, or
    a mixture
2 large slices of country-style or
    sourdough bread
100g (about ¾ cup) sauerkraut,
    or to taste
150g (5½oz) ham, chopped or sliced

Melt the butter in a small pan, then add the garlic clove. Reduce the heat and cook gently until the garlic is pale gold. Scoop out and discard.

Add the flour to the garlicky butter and stir over a medium heat for 2 minutes. Take the pan off the heat and gradually pour in the milk, stirring all the time. Stir in the wine, mustard and nutmeg. Return the pan to a medium heat and cook, stirring constantly, for 2–3 minutes until smooth and creamy.

Add half the cheese and, when melted, take the pan off the heat. Now, set your grill (broiler) on high.

Spread both sides of the bread with the extra butter and place in a large ovenproof frying pan (skillet) over a medium heat. Fry on both sides until golden. (Alternatively, use a non-ovenproof pan then transfer the bread to a baking sheet lined with baking paper.)

Top each fried slice of bread with half the sauerkraut and the ham. Divide the sauce between the slices and spread it out (it will spread further once under the grill). Sprinkle with the remaining cheese.

Grill until bubbling and golden in patches, about 5 minutes. Serve immediately with a sharply dressed salad.

Try...
Using kimchi instead of sauerkraut. You could also pop a fried egg on top to make it a croque madame.

What about...
Rustling up a jambon-beurre if you have some really tasty leftover ham? This classic French sandwich is simple but unbeatable if your ingredients are good. Slice a hunk of fresh baguette lengthways and spread (thickly, if you're like me) with quality salted butter. Fill with thinly sliced ham and nothing else. Bliss.

Cheese *and* chutney puff pastry tart

This tart is divine: creamy, cheesy loveliness inside a flaky pastry case, with sharp pickles to cut the richness. It's ideal for using up scraps of cheese – see my tip below. I've specified puff pastry here, because the light buttery crust works brilliantly with the rich filling, but do use shortcrust if you prefer.

Leftovers: bits and bobs of cheese, fresh herbs

Serves 4–6
Preparation: 10 minutes
Cooking: 1 hour

1 sheet ready-rolled puff pastry
125ml (½ cup) full-fat (whole) milk
125ml (½ cup) double (heavy) cream
3 large eggs
200g (about 2 cups) grated or crumbled cheese, plus extra for sprinkling
2 Tbsp finely chopped fresh chives, parsley or other herbs, plus extra for sprinkling
3–4 Tbsp chutney or pickles (see tip below)
Fine sea salt and freshly ground black pepper

Line and grease a 23cm (9in) loose-bottomed tart tin with the pastry, pressing it gently but firmly into the edges. Trim off any excess (freeze for later – see the ideas on page 177) and prick the base all over with a fork. Chill for 20 minutes.

Preheat the oven to 200°C/180°C fan/400°F/Gas mark 6 and place a baking sheet inside. Crumple a sheet of baking paper, uncrumple it, then use it to line the pastry case. Fill with ceramic baking beans (or dried beans or rice), making sure they cover the base right up to the edge. Transfer to the hot baking sheet and bake for 15 minutes. Remove the paper and beans/rice and bake for a further 10–15 minutes, until firm and pale gold.

Meanwhile, beat together the milk, cream, eggs, cheese and herbs with a fork. Season generously with salt and pepper.

Remove the tart case from the oven on its baking sheet – it will make it easier to transfer back to the oven when filled. Don't worry if the base has puffed up a bit – just press down gently with your hand protected with a clean tea towel (dish towel). Spread a thin layer of chutney over the base of the tart case, then pour in the filling. Sprinkle the top with the extra cheese. Bake for 25–30 minutes or until just set (the middle will still be slightly wobbly), then scatter with chives.

Try ...

Including a mix of cheeses, at least one with good flavour that melts well, like strong Cheddar, Lancashire, Gruyère, Comté or Taleggio, as well as a little punchy stuff like blue or Parmesan. Pizza mozzarella (the drier grated stuff, not fresh) is great for meltiness, but don't use more than a quarter of the total amount, as the tart might be too oozy to cut.

Using up those near-empty chutney jars loitering in the fridge. Fruity chutneys are fantastic – mango, fig or apple, for example. Finely chopped pickled walnuts scattered over the base of the tart work incredibly well too, as do caramelized onions from a jar.

Tender baked halloumi *with* chimichurri

If you're a bit unsure about halloumi due to its rubbery, squeaky character, try cooking it this way. It's amazing. Frying it first creates a golden outer crust, then roasting it whole delivers a juicy and fudge-soft inner texture. Paired with chimichurri, a punchy Latin American sauce, this dish takes care of any half-used packs or bunches of soft herbs – both leaves and fine stalks – and is perfect as a light lunch. Thanks to Dorset-based chef Jesse Wells at Terroir Tapas for the inspiration and halloumi chat.

Leftovers: fresh herbs, chillies

Serves 4
Preparation: 15 minutes plus
 10 minutes soaking
Cooking: 18 minutes

2 blocks of halloumi
About 130ml (generous ½ cup) olive
 oil, more or less as needed
A handful of fresh herbs and tender
 stalks: parsley, coriander (cilantro),
 dill, mint, chervil, basil
1 medium red chilli, deseeded and
 roughly chopped
1 large garlic clove, roughly chopped
¼ tsp dried oregano or mixed herbs
1 Tbsp red wine vinegar or sherry
 vinegar, or more to taste
1 Tbsp lemon or lime juice, plus extra
 as needed
Fine sea salt

Preheat the oven to 200°C/180°C fan/400°F/Gas mark 6. Place the halloumi blocks in a bowl of cold water and soak for 10 minutes to tenderize and reduce saltiness. Pat dry with paper towel.

Set an ovenproof frying pan (skillet), ideally non-stick, over a medium-high heat. When hot, add 2 tablespoons of the oil and fry the halloumi blocks on one of their large sides until golden. Fry all the small sides until golden, leaving one large side uncooked.

With the uncooked sides pan-side down, transfer the halloumi to the oven and bake for 18 minutes, until very soft. Start checking after 15 minutes.

Meanwhile, make the chimichurri. Very finely chop the fresh herbs and place in a bowl with the chilli, garlic and oregano. Add the vinegar, then gradually stir in the remaining oil to make a very loose sauce – you might not need all the oil. Add the lemon juice and taste; stir in more lemon juice, salt or oil if needed.

Serve the halloumi hot (don't hang about, as it firms up quickly as it cools) with the chimichurri spooned over.

Try ...
Serving chimichurri on eggs, fish, steak, chicken – or stir through soup and stews to ramp up the flavour. It tastes best when it's made fresh for the dish.

Main Meals

Lemony yoghurt pasta *with* chicken *and* za'atar

A quick, simple and vibrant way to enjoy leftover chicken. I've specified 200g (7oz) of chicken but if you don't have that much, this dish is accommodating and will be delicious with however much you have. It's also lovely with leftover turkey, so bookmark for Christmas or Thanksgiving. Za'atar is an incredible spice mixture that's widely available in supermarkets, but I've included a recipe below if you would like to make your own.

Leftovers: cooked chicken

Serves 4
Preparation: 15 minutes

350g (12oz) uncooked spaghetti or
   linguine
1 Tbsp olive oil, plus extra for the pasta
   if needed
150g (⅔ cup) butter
1 onion, finely chopped
Fine sea salt
2 garlic cloves, finely chopped
Finely grated zest and juice of ½ lemon
2 Tbsp za'atar (see below)
200g (7oz) cooked chicken, chopped
   or shredded
300g (1½ cups) Greek yoghurt
30g (¼ cup) pine nuts, toasted
A handful of parsley leaves, chopped
   (optional)

For the za'atar
50g (about ½ cup) pistachios or
   almonds
 1 Tbsp sesame seeds
1 heaped Tbsp dried oregano
1 Tbsp sumac
½ tsp sea salt flakes

If you're making your own za'atar, roughly chop the pistachios or almonds, add to a dry frying pan with the sesame seeds and lightly toast. Tip into a bowl and stir in the dried oregano, sumac and sea salt flakes. Set aside, and store any leftovers in an airtight jar or bag for 3–6 months.

Cook the pasta in boiling salted water for 1 minute less than the packet instructions. Drain in a colander (strainer) and reserve a mugful of the cooking water. If the pasta is ready before the sauce is cooked, toss it with a splash of olive oil and set aside.

Meanwhile, heat the olive oil and a tablespoonful of the butter in a large frying pan (skillet). Gently fry the onion with a pinch of salt until soft and translucent, about 8 minutes. Add the garlic, lemon zest and juice and za'atar. Fry, stirring, for 1 minute.

Add the rest of the butter to the pan and, when melted, add the chicken. Turn to coat in the lemony butter and onions, then cook for long enough to warm it through. Add the pasta and toss well.

Over a low heat, stir through the yoghurt and half the pine nuts. Add as much of the reserved cooking water as you need to make a loose creamy sauce. Serve immediately with the remaining pine nuts and parsley (if using) scattered over the top.

Lime *and* chilli chicken salad *with* crispy noodles

The recipe for this deeply delicious and sprightly Thai-flavoured salad is based on one by Australian chef Simmone Logue in her book *In The Kitchen*. It's reason enough to cook a chicken – perfect for the lunchbox or supper the day after a roast dinner, and amazingly flexible in terms of ingredients. The dressing might involve planning ahead and buying in a couple of specialist ingredients, but this is a real celebration of leftovers and well worth it.

Leftovers: cooked chicken, raw veg

Serves 2 generously as a main
Preparation: 20 minutes

150g (5½oz) medium fresh egg noodles (the straight-to-wok kind)
A splash of sesame oil or vegetable oil
Fine sea salt

For the dressing
4cm (1½in) piece of root ginger, grated
1 red chilli (medium heat), sliced
1 lemongrass stalk, white part only, grated
1 garlic clove, peeled
2 spring onions (scallions), chopped
Finely grated zest and juice of 2 limes, or more to taste
1 Tbsp sweet chilli sauce
2 Tbsp fish sauce
2 Tbsp soy sauce
A handful of coriander (cilantro) leaves, roughly chopped
A handful of mint leaves, chopped
4 Tbsp vegetable oil or other flavourless oil, or more if needed

For the salad
A handful of cooked chicken, chopped or shredded
4 handfuls of crisp raw veg (about 600g/1lb 5oz): beansprouts, mangetout (sugar snap peas), chopped cucumber, chopped red (bell) pepper, cherry tomatoes, grated carrot, finely sliced cabbage
A handful of coriander leaves

Preheat the oven to 180°C/160°C fan/350°F/Gas mark 4 and line a baking sheet with baking paper.

Separate the noodles, drizzle with the sesame oil and toss with your hands to coat. Spread out in a single layer on the prepared baking sheet – you want them as far apart as possible. Roast for 15 minutes or so, turning every 5 minutes, until crispy and golden. Sprinkle with salt, leave to cool and break up a little.

Meanwhile, put all the dressing ingredients in the bowl of a food processor or blender and blitz until smooth. It should have the consistency of double (heavy) cream, so adjust with more oil or lime juice to achieve the right consistency and taste.

Combine all the salad ingredients in a bowl and toss with enough dressing to coat everything well.

Serve immediately, with the crispy noodles and any extra dressing alongside.

Try ...
Using leftover lamb, beef or pork instead of chicken.

Swap ...
The vegetables suggested with whatever you like or need to use up, so long as they have some crunch.

Add ...
Toasted chopped peanuts or sesame seeds if you like.

Spatchcock chicken *with* roasted fruit

Not everyone is in favour of a meat and fruit partnership, but this dish might persuade them. It's a perfect way to use up very soft and very hard fruit, including specimens that won't ripen. Roasting the bird on top of the fruit makes for succulent meat and generates a delicious gravy that carries a hint of fruity sweetness.

Leftovers: stone fruit, apples and pears that need using up

Serves 4–6
Preparation: 30 minutes
Cooking: 1–1¼ hours

1 whole medium or large chicken
3 Tbsp butter
1 Tbsp olive oil
1 Tbsp honey
5–6 firm stone fruit or pears or bruised/soft apples
2 onions, quartered
1 head of garlic, halved horizontally
1 rosemary sprig
2 bay leaves
700ml (3 cups) hot chicken stock
4 Tbsp plain (all-purpose) flour
4 Tbsp white wine
Fine sea salt and freshly ground black pepper

Preheat the oven to 180°C/160°C fan/350°F/Gas mark 4.

To spatchcock (butterfly) the chicken, place on a chopping board with the backbone facing upwards. Using kitchen scissors, cut down both sides of the backbone and remove it (reserve for chicken stock). Turn the chicken over and push down to flatten. Set aside.

Set a roasting tray large enough to fit the chicken snugly over a medium heat. Add the butter, olive oil and honey. Allow to melt, stir, then take off the heat. Brush the chicken generously with the mixture and season generously with salt and pepper.

Halve and remove the stones from stone fruit (if using). Halve and core the pears or apples (cut into quarters if large), cutting off any bruised bits. Add the fruit, onions and garlic to the roasting tray, and turn to coat in the butter. Tuck in the rosemary and bay leaves, and season with salt and pepper. Place the chicken on top of the fruit and onions. Pour in 250ml (generous 1 cup) of the stock and roast for 1–1¼ hours, or until the juices run clear when you pierce the thigh with a knife.

Transfer the chicken to a plate, along with half the fruit and onions, leaving the softest pieces in the tray. Squeeze the garlic cloves into the tray, discarding the skins, and roughly mash everything with a fork or potato masher. Set the tray over a low heat and sprinkle over the flour. Cook, stirring for a couple of minutes, then add the wine. Let it bubble up and reduce a bit, then add the remaining stock. Simmer, stirring, for 5 minutes.

Pour the contents of the roasting tray through a sieve set over a jug. Press down on the fruit and onions to squeeze out as much liquid as possible. Return the gravy to the roasting tray. If too thin, reduce a little more, and add any juices that have collected under the chicken. Serve the chicken with the roast fruit and onions, and the gravy on the side.

Chicken in milk *with* ras el hanout *and* garlic

I've been pot-roasting meat, including pork and goat, in milk (and coconut milk) for years, and I adore it. Here I've opted for chicken. The meat turns beautifully tender, and the milk transforms into a rich sauce imbued with flavour from meat juices. This dish is terrific for using up leftover milk (especially stuff that has just gone past its best-before date). The milk will curdle but that's as it should be – the sauce will be utterly delicious.

Leftover: milk

Serves 4
Preparation: about 1 hour

8 chicken thighs, skin on, bone in
50g (about ½ cup) cornflour
  (cornstarch)
2 Tbsp vegetable oil, plus extra if
  needed
25g (3 Tbsp) butter
6 large garlic cloves, crushed
1½ Tbsp ras el hanout
600ml (generous 2½ cups) full-fat
  (whole) milk
Lemon juice, to taste
Fine sea salt and freshly ground
  black pepper
Rice or mashed potato, to serve
Greens, to serve

Pat dry the chicken thighs with paper towel and generously season with salt.

Spread the flour on a plate and season with salt and pepper. Dredge the thighs in the flour to coat thoroughly, shaking off any excess.

Heat the oil in a heavy frying pan (skillet). Working in batches, brown the chicken all over, transferring the thighs to a plate as you go. With the pan over a medium heat, melt the butter. Add the garlic and ras el hanout and stir for 30 seconds, then stir in the milk. Return the chicken to the pan and simmer gently, uncovered, for 40 minutes. Turn the chicken now again and stir the milk to prevent it catching on the bottom of the pan.

If the milk is starting to reduce too much before the chicken is cooked, half-cover the pan with the lid. Check for doneness by slicing into one of the thighs with a sharp knife – if the meat is no longer pink, it's cooked.

Squeeze over lemon juice and taste the sauce: add more seasoning if needed. Serve immediately, with the rice or mashed potato and a bowl of greens.

Chilli beef *with* red beans *and* smoky Cheddar cobbler

Leftover cooked beef is reimagined into a glorious rib-sticking stew that delivers comfort and joy on a cold winter's night. There's a hint of cocoa in here for richness, some spice for gentle heat, red beans to bolster and cheesy 'scones' to soak up the sauce.

Leftovers: roast beef

Serves 4–6
Preparation: 45 minutes
Cooking: 30 minutes

4 Tbsp vegetable oil
300g (10½oz) cooked beef, cut into
    1.5cm (⅝in) cubes
2 Tbsp sriracha sauce
1 onion, finely chopped
2 garlic cloves, finely chopped
1½ tsp each ground cumin and hot
    chilli powder
½ tsp each ground cinnamon and
    cocoa powder
½ tsp dried oregano
1 red chilli (medium heat), finely sliced
1 x 400g (14oz) can chopped tomatoes
250ml (generous 1 cup) beef stock
500g (1lb 2oz) drained canned kidney,
    borlotti, black or aduki beans
A squeeze of lime
Fine sea salt

For the cheese cobbler
175g (1⅓ cups) self-raising (self-rising)
    flour, plus extra for dusting
¾ tsp baking powder
A pinch of smoked paprika
75g (about ¾ cup) grated
    strong Cheddar
100ml (¾ cup plus 2 Tbsp) milk
    (more as needed)
1 egg, beaten

Place a heavy 25cm (10in) ovenproof casserole over a high heat and, when hot, add 2 tablespoons of the oil. Add the meat and fry for 2 minutes, stirring now and then but leaving it undisturbed for long enough to get good colour. Add the sriracha and fry for another 2 minutes. Remove to a bowl with a slotted spoon.

Warm the remaining oil in the same pan (wipe it out first if the sriracha has caught too much or burned on the bottom). Add the onion and gently fry with a pinch of salt until soft and golden. Add the garlic and cook for 2 minutes more.

Stir in the spices, cocoa powder, oregano and sliced red chilli. Fry over a medium heat for another couple of minutes. Stir in the tomatoes and then the stock. Let the liquid bubble away gently until thickened and reduced by about a quarter. Gently stir in the meat and beans. There should be just enough sauce to cover them, so gently simmer to reduce a little more if necessary then set aside.

Preheat the oven to 220°C/200°C fan/425°F/Gas mark 7. Place all the cobbler ingredients except the milk and egg in a bowl and mix well with your hands. Gradually add the milk, mixing between each addition, to make a shaggy and only slightly sticky dough.

Knead briefly on a lightly floured work surface. Pat into a disc about 1cm (⅝in) thick and stamp out circles using a cookie cutter or a glass dipped in flour (6cm/2½in diameter is ideal). Re-roll the trimmings and continue stamping out and rolling until all the dough is used up and you've made about 10 'cobblers'.

Brush the tops with beaten egg, then arrange the cobblers on top of the chilli. Quickly but carefully transfer to the oven and bake for 25–30 minutes until the cobblers are risen and golden. Serve immediately.

Salad leaf pesto *with* broccoli, mint *and* pistachios

Assemble your leftover salad greens, herbs and nuts plus a floret or two of broccoli and you've got yourself a tasty sauce for pasta. I've specified mint and pistachios because they're a fun couple, but basil, dill or even parsley are genial too. If you don't fancy pasta, use the pesto as a dressing for potato salad, or serve it as a relish for fish, chicken or lamb chops. It's also great smothered on a cold meat sandwich.

Leftovers: salad leaves, herbs, broccoli

Serves 2
Preparation: 10 minutes
Cooking: about 10 minutes

200g (7oz) uncooked pasta
100g (3½oz) cooked broccoli, very
  finely chopped

For the pesto
30g (about 3 Tbsp) pistachios, toasted
1 garlic clove, roughly chopped
25g (1oz) mint leaves
A handful (about 20g/¾oz) lettuce or
  mixed salad leaves
15g (about 3 Tbsp) grated Parmesan,
  plus extra to serve
Grated zest and juice of ½ lemon,
  plus extra juice to taste
120ml (½ cup) olive oil, plus extra if
  needed
A pinch of fine sea salt

Cook the pasta in boiling salted water according to the packet instructions.

Meanwhile, put all the ingredients for the pesto in the bowl of a food processer and pulse to make a chunky emerald-green sauce flecked with nuts. Pour into a bowl and stir in the broccoli. Taste and add more lemon juice, salt or olive oil to taste.

Drain the pasta, return to the pan and toss with the pesto. Serve immediately, sprinkled with Parmesan.

Try ...
Adding other flavours into the pesto. Mix in 1 Tbsp finely chopped capers (rinsed well if packed in salt), or 1 Tbsp finely chopped preserved lemon or 2–3 finely chopped cornichons. If you like heat, 1 Tbsp chopped red or green chilli is also a great addition.

Peanut *and* tamarind vegetable curry *with* mint *and* dates

I often roast a couple of trays of veg on a Sunday specifically to eat for supper during the week – this dish is one I often use them in. But any leftover veg can be given a glow-up in this tangy, fruity curry. The sweet-sour notes of the tamarind complement root veg perfectly, but any sturdy cooked veg works well. If you don't have quite enough, top up with frozen peas.

Leftovers: cooked vegetables

Serves 4
Preparation: 40 minutes

2 Tbsp vegetable oil
1 onion, finely chopped
1 tsp mustard seeds
1 tsp ground cinnamon
1 tsp ground cumin
4cm (1½in) piece of root ginger, grated
2 red chillies, finely sliced
2 Tbsp tomato purée (paste)
2 Tbsp tamarind purée (paste)
1 x 400g (14oz) can chopped tomatoes
1 Tbsp soft light brown sugar
70g (about ½ cup) toasted peanuts,
    roughly chopped
8 dates, halved and pitted
500g (1lb 2oz) cooked vegetables,
    cut into 3cm (1¼in) chunks
Fine sea salt
Boiled or steamed long-grain rice,
    to serve

Warm the oil in a large frying pan (skillet) and fry the onion with a pinch of salt until soft and translucent, about 8 minutes. Add the spices and cook for a few minutes more.

Add the ginger and chillies and fry until fragrant, then stir in the tomato and tamarind purées (pastes). Fry for 1 minute.

Add the tomatoes, sugar and ¼ teaspoon of salt. Simmer over a medium heat for a few minutes until thickened to a rich sauce. Stir in the peanuts and dates. Taste and adjust for salt or sugar – the sauce should have a good balance of sweet and salty.

Add the cooked veg and cook gently until warmed through. Serve with the rice.

Vegetable *and* white bean stew *with* charred tomatoes, yoghurt *and* paprika oil

This gentle dish of placidly simmered vegetables is boosted by blackened tomatoes and a little spice. Although filling and comforting, it's also light and bright, as most of the vegetables, ideally, retain a bit of bite. It sounds like a very worthy dish (and yes it is good for you) but it is also deeply tasty.

Forage in your salad crisper drawer and store cupboard for vegetables that need using up. Weigh them together, then separate into sturdy, medium, soft and leafy veg, as they're best cooked for different amounts of time (see below for guidance). Cut them into very small chunks and finely slice leafy greens, such as cabbage and kale. You can also add cooked veg into the mix at the end.

Leftovers: odds and ends of cooked and uncooked vegetables

Serves 4–6
Preparation: about 1 hour

250g (9oz) cherry tomatoes
3 Tbsp olive oil
1 onion or small leek, finely sliced
1 carrot, finely chopped (optional)
1 celery stick, finely sliced (optional)
3 large garlic cloves, finely chopped
2 tsp chilli paste, such as harissa or
    chipotle, or ½ tsp chilli flakes
1 heaped tsp dried oregano
About 500g (1lb 2oz) mixed veg, cooked
    and uncooked, chopped small or, for
    greens, finely sliced
500g (1lb 2oz) drained white beans
    from cans or jars, liquid reserved
300ml (1¼ cups plus 1 Tbsp) vegetable
    or chicken stock
A handful of fresh soft herbs, such as
    basil, parsley, coriander (cilantro)
    or mint
Lemon juice, to taste
Fine sea salt and freshly ground
    black pepper
120g (generous ½ cup) Greek yoghurt,
    to serve

For the paprika oil
90ml (generous ⅓ cup) olive oil
1 tsp smoked paprika
A pinch of cayenne

Fry the tomatoes in a large dry frying pan (skillet), shaking often, until charred and blistered. Transfer to a bowl with any juices.

Wipe out the pan, add the olive oil and gently fry the onion, carrot and celery with a pinch of salt until very soft for 10–15 minutes.

Add the garlic, chilli paste, oregano and some black pepper, and stir-fry for 1 minute. Add any sturdy veg and briefly stir-fry over a high heat. Reduce the heat to low, add a generous splash of water, and cover. Cook until the veg are almost tender, stirring often to prevent sticking. Add a splash more water if needed.

Meanwhile, take half the beans and their liquid and blitz to a purée or mash with a fork. Set aside.

Add any medium veg to the pan and cook as for the sturdy veg until just tender, then add the unmashed beans, soft veg, leafy veg and cooked vegetables. Stir in the stock and puréed or mashed beans. Gently simmer until everything is warmed through and the beans are soft, about 10 minutes. Add the charred tomatoes.

Meanwhile make the paprika oil. Pour the oil into a small pan and add the paprika and cayenne. Gently warm until the oil smells delicious – be careful not to let it burn.

Add the herbs and lemon juice to the vegetables. Taste and add more salt and pepper if needed. Ladle into bowls and serve topped with yoghurt and a drizzle of paprika oil.

Sturdy veg: root veg, such as carrots, potatoes, turnips, swede (rutabaga), parsnips, and winter squash.
Medium veg: broccoli, cauliflower, Brussels sprouts, cabbage.
Soft veg: courgettes (zucchini), peppers, mushrooms, cooked veg.
Leafy veg: cabbage, kale, spinach, Swiss chard, lettuce, pak choi (bok choy), endive salad leaves, rocket (arugula), watercress.

Pomegranate lamb *and* lentils *with* preserved lemon white bean mash

Sometimes we veer away from leftovers because we think we don't want to eat the same thing more than once in quick succession. But the 'not-again' syndrome doesn't apply with this dish, which transforms leftover meat into something that tastes entirely different from the way it did first time around. The intense tangy sauce bathes roast lamb that is crisped up – roast beef will also work. Lentils bulk out the stew deliciously; in fact, if you're short on meat, just add more lentils.

Leftovers: roast lamb or beef, preserved lemon

Serves 4
Preparation: 30 minutes

For the sauce
150g (5½oz) tomato purée (paste)
3 Tbsp pomegranate molasses
3 Tbsp pul biber
1½ Tbsp dried oregano
3 Tbsp runny honey
¾ tsp fine sea salt
About 250g (9oz) cooked drained Puy
   or green lentils from a can or pouch

For the white bean purée
200ml (scant 1 cup) chicken or
   vegetable stock
2 x 400g (14oz) cans white beans
   (butter/lima or cannellini), rinsed
2 garlic cloves, chopped
1 small preserved lemon, finely chopped
3 Tbsp olive oil, plus extra as needed
¼ tsp fine sea salt
Juice of ½ lemon, or to taste

For the lamb
1 Tbsp olive oil, plus a splash more as
   needed
500g (1lb 2oz) cooked lamb (ideally
   include some pink meat as well as
   fatty bits), cut into bite-sized chunks

Chopped fresh coriander (cilantro),
   to serve

For the sauce, put all the ingredients except the lentils in a small pan with 300ml (1¼ cups plus 1 Tbsp) water and stir well. Simmer gently for a couple of minutes until thickened slightly. Add the lentils and continue simmering until the lentils are warmed through. Take the pan off the heat.

For the purée, tip all the ingredients, except the lemon juice, into a second pan and simmer over a medium-low heat for 3 minutes. Strain, reserving the cooking liquid, and blitz in a food processor until smooth and creamy. Loosen with some of the reserved cooking liquid if it's too stiff. Return the purée to the pan and add the lemon juice and seasoning to taste. Keep warm while you fry the lamb.

Heat a frying pan (skillet) until very hot, add the oil and then the lamb. Fry for about 5 minutes, shaking the pan now and then but leave the lamb undisturbed for long enough to brown and crisp up. You're looking for meat that's deeply burnished on the outside (be careful not to let it burn) but not dried out. Add a splash more oil if it starts to stick to the pan.

When the lamb is done, take the pan off the heat and add the lentil sauce – it will bubble up. Stir, scraping up any crispy bits, and return to a low heat to reduce a little.

Serve the meat and sauce with a scoop of purée, sprinkled with coriander.

Ham, cabbage, apple *and* mustard gratin

This is such a delicious way to use up ham – it's rich, certainly, but the apple offers bright contrast to the cream and salty meat. You could serve this as a side dish but I think it's a main meal, a centrepiece all on its own.

Leftovers: ham

Serves 4
Preparation: 20 minutes
Cooking: 25 minutes

400ml (1¾ cups) single (light) cream
1 garlic clove, flattened with the side
  of a knife
2 thyme sprigs
2 tsp Dijon mustard
400g (14oz) Savoy or sweetheart
  (Hispi) cabbage leaves, sliced
40g (about ½ cup) dried breadcrumbs
15g (about 3 Tbsp) finely grated
  Parmesan
3 Tbsp olive oil
1 Tbsp butter, plus extra for greasing
1 onion, finely chopped
1 large apple
100g (3½oz) cooked ham, chopped
40g (scant ½ cup) grated strong
  Cheddar
Fine sea salt

Put the cream, garlic and thyme in a small pan and very gently simmer for 8 minutes. Take the pan off the heat and stir in the mustard. Set aside.

Meanwhile, blanch the cabbage in boiling salted water for 3 minutes. Drain and reserve a cup of the cooking water. When cool enough to handle, squeeze out any excess water.

Mix together the breadcrumbs, Parmesan and 1 tablespoon of the olive oil. Set aside.

In a large frying pan (skillet), melt the butter and the rest of the oil. Gently fry the onion with a pinch of salt until soft and translucent, about 8 minutes.

Preheat the oven to 200°C/180°C fan/400°F/Gas mark 6 and butter a 2-litre (70fl oz) baking dish.

Peel, core and chop the apple into small chunks. Add the apple and cabbage to the onion pan and stir to combine. Fry for a minute or so, then take the pan off the heat and mix in the ham and Cheddar. If the cream has thickened too much to pour easily, add a splash or two of the reserved cabbage water to loosen – it should still be the consistency of single (light) cream. Remove the thyme sprigs from the cream, stir into the cabbage mixture, then spoon into the prepared baking dish. Sprinkle over the prepared breadcrumbs. Bake for 25–30 minutes or until golden and bubbling.

Lamb *and* pumpkin pilaf *with* pumpkin seeds, mint *and* yoghurt

This dish is a true celebration of leftovers. I've made this magnificent meal using leftover lamb shank, leg and shoulder and they all work well – just avoid overly fatty pieces and use pink meat if you can. The toasted pumpkin seeds deliver wonderful toasted notes.

Leftovers: cooked lamb

Serves 4
Preparation: 30 minutes
Cooking: 1 hour 10 minutes

400g (14oz) peeled and deseeded
  butternut squash (or winter
  pumpkin), cut into 1.5cm (⅝in)
  chunks
3 Tbsp olive oil
300g (generous 1½ cups) basmati rice
1 onion, chopped
2 garlic cloves, chopped
8 cardamom pods, crushed
1 cinnamon stick
2 strips of orange zest
350g (12oz) cooked lamb, cut into
  bite-sized chunks
40g (about ¼ cup) dried cherries
700ml (3 cups) chicken or vegetable
  stock
3 Tbsp pumpkin seed oil (or olive oil
  is fine)
4 Tbsp pumpkin seeds
A handful of fresh mint leaves,
  finely chopped
Fine sea salt and freshly ground
  black pepper
Greek yoghurt, to serve

Preheat the oven to 180°C/160°C fan/350°F/Gas mark 4.

Spread out the squash in a large roasting tray, drizzle with 1 tablespoon of the oil and season with salt and pepper. Toss to coat and then roast for 30–40 minutes, or until the chunks are tender and golden at the edges. Meanwhile, soak the rice in cold water.

Warm the remaining oil in a large, lidded ovenproof pan (I use a 23cm/9in) casserole) and fry the onion over a low heat until soft and translucent, 8–10 minutes. Stir in the garlic, spices and orange zest and cook for 2 minutes more. Add the lamb and cook for a few minutes over a medium heat, stirring, so any fat in the lamb melts.

Drain and rinse the rice, then drain again and add to the pan with the lamb. Add the dried cherries, stock and ¼ teaspoon of salt. Bring to the boil then reduce the heat to low and cover. If your lid doesn't have an air vent, drape a clean tea towel (dish towel) over the pan and place the lid on top – this stops condensation dripping back into the rice which hinders steaming. Cook for 20–30 minutes or until the liquid is absorbed and the rice tender.

Meanwhile, warm the pumpkin seed oil in a small frying pan (skillet), add the pumpkin seeds, and gently fry until lightly toasted – they'll start to pop and jump. Remove from the heat.

When the rice is done, tip onto a serving platter and gently fold in the squash, half the mint and half the pumpkin seeds. Sprinkle over the remaining mint, pumpkin seeds and any oil from the frying pan.

Serve immediately, with Greek yoghurt on the side.

Swap ...
Beef for lamb. Use coriander (cilantro) instead of or as well as mint. Sultanas (golden raisins), dried apricots or cranberries work beautifully instead of cherries.

Try ...
Adding salad greens or spinach leaves that need using up. Slice finely and fold through the finished pilaf and leave to sit for a few minutes before serving. The leaves will wilt in the residual heat.

Roast dinner enchiladas

Often, there's not enough left of any one ingredient after a roast dinner to pull together a whole new meal – you've just got scraps of meat and vegetables. These enchiladas are the perfect carrier for whatever's left – gently spicy, filling and comforting. Use whatever jumble of cheeses you have in the fridge, too.

Leftovers: cooked vegetables, cooked meat, cooked sausages, odds and ends of cheese

Serves 4–6
Preparation: 40 minutes
Cooking: 25 minutes

500–600g (1lb 2oz–1lb 5oz) leftover cooked meat and/or vegetables, chopped
200g (about 2 cups) grated hard cheese, such as Cheddar, Parmesan, Gruyère, Lancashire or a mix
4 large tortilla wraps

For the tomato sauce
2 Tbsp olive oil, plus extra for brushing
1 large onion, finely chopped
2 garlic cloves, finely chopped
2 Tbsp chilli powder
2 Tbsp smoked paprika
1 Tbsp ground cumin
1 tsp dried oregano
2 tsp brown sugar
1 tsp fine sea salt
2 x 400g (14oz) cans chopped tomatoes

For the sauce, warm the oil in a large frying pan (skillet) and fry the onion until soft and golden, about 8 minutes. Add the garlic and cook for 1 minute. Add the spices, oregano, sugar and salt and cook gently, stirring, for a further minute.

Add the tomatoes and simmer gently for 15 minutes, stirring now and again, until you have a rich, thick, deep-red sauce. Taste, add more salt if needed, then take the pan off the heat.

Meanwhile, preheat the oven to 180°C/160°C fan/350°F/Gas mark 4 and brush a baking dish measuring about 20cm (8in) square with olive oil.

Distribute the leftovers and half the cheese equally between the wraps and roll them up. Arrange in the prepared baking dish – they should fit snugly. Spoon the tomato sauce between and over the wraps. Sprinkle the remaining cheese on top. Bake for 20–25 minutes until golden and bubbling. Serve hot with salad on the side.

Chilli- *and* lime-caramel pork *with* rice noodles *and* sesame

Leftover roast pork belly or shoulder is ideal for this divine noodle dish; it's salty, sweet, intensely savoury and popping with a hint of lime. Rich and fatty, the pork reheats beautifully, with some bits crisping up and others remaining succulent and meaty. I've specified quantities to serve two but scale up as your leftovers allow.

Leftovers: roast pork belly or shoulder

Serves 2
Preparation: 15 minutes

100g (3½oz) thin dried egg noodles
A splash of sesame oil
Vegetable oil, for frying
250g (9oz) leftover cooked pork,
    cut into small chunks

For the caramel
2 Tbsp soft brown sugar
1½ Tbsp runny honey
1 Tbsp sesame oil
1 Tbsp vegetable oil
1½ Tbsp fish sauce
1½ Tbsp lime juice
½ Tbsp light soy sauce
1 red chilli (medium heat), finely sliced
1 small garlic clove, finely chopped

To serve
1 Tbsp sesame seeds
Steamed pak choi (bok choy) or
    other greens

Cook the noodles according to the packet instructions. Drain, rinse in cold water and drain again. Use your hands to toss with a splash of sesame oil to separate the strands. Set aside.

For the caramel, put all the ingredients in a small pan with 2 tablespoons of water. Stir well and set aside so it's ready to cook when the pork is done.

Warm a splash of vegetable oil in a large frying pan (skillet). This is to start the pork off, but it will release its own fat, so you don't need much. Cook over a medium-low heat at first, to allow the fat in the pork to melt. Increase the heat to medium-high and stir-fry, breaking up some of the pieces with the side of a spoon to get a mixture of shreds and chunks. Keep scraping up the crispy bits from the bottom of the pan so they don't burn. When the pork is golden in parts and sizzling, place the pan half-on the lowest heat possible, just to keep warm.

Cook the caramel gently over a low heat until the sugar dissolves. Increase the heat and simmer until the mixture has thickened slightly into a thin syrup.

Add the noodles and caramel to the pan with the pork and toss to combine. Sprinkle with sesame seeds and serve immediately with pak choi (bok choy) or other greens.

Smoky Cajun-inspired rice

This is closely based on jambalaya, a treasured Cajun/Creole dish that my husband loves and has been cooking for years. This version is by no means authentic because I've adapted it to use leftovers. But it's a dream come true for the remains of Christmas or Thanksgiving lunch because you can use up so many of the components.

Leftovers: cooked chicken, turkey, pork, ham, sausages

Serves 4
Preparation: about 1 hour

About 250g (9oz) sausages (cooked or uncooked) and/or bacon and/or ham
2 Tbsp goose or duck fat, dripping or vegetable oil (if needed)
1 large onion, finely chopped
1 red or green (bell) pepper, finely chopped
2 celery sticks, finely chopped
2 spring onions (scallions), finely chopped
2 garlic cloves, finely chopped
2 Tbsp tomato purée (paste)
1 x 400g (14oz) can chopped tomatoes
1 tsp dried thyme
1 tsp ground black pepper
2 tsp smoked paprika
½ tsp cayenne pepper
200g (generous 1 cup) long-grain rice, rinsed well and drained
700ml (3 cups) chicken or turkey stock, or more as needed
About 250g (9oz) cooked chicken, turkey and/or pork, cut into bite-sized chunks
Fine sea salt
Hot sauce, to serve

Place the uncooked sausages and bacon (if using) in a heavy casserole over a medium heat. A bit of the fat from both will come out as they warm up but if the pan stays dry, add some extra fat. Turn to coat in the hot fat, then keep cooking and turning now and then until cooked through. The bacon should take 2–4 minutes each side – remove from the pan when done. The sausages will take 15–20 minutes. Cut into bite-sized pieces and transfer to a plate with the chopped cooked sausages and any ham you're adding to the dish. Set aside.

Pour the fat from the pan into a bowl, then add back 2 tablespoons (or if there's not enough, use dripping or oil).

Add the onion, (bell) pepper, celery, spring onions (scallions) and a generous pinch of salt to the pan and fry gently over a medium-low heat for 15 minutes until soft and translucent. Stir in the garlic and tomato purée (paste) and fry for 3 more minutes or until you can smell the tomato caramelizing.

Stir in the canned tomatoes, thyme and spices and simmer for 5 minutes over a medium heat.

Stir in the rice and stock. Bring to a simmer, then reduce the heat to medium-low, cover and cook for 10 minutes, stirring regularly to ensure the rice doesn't stick. Fold in the meat, and cook for a further 10 minutes, covered, again stirring regularly. If the rice is not done after 20 minutes total cooking, add a splash more stock or water and continue cooking until the rice is tender; you want quite a loose consistency.

Serve immediately, with your favourite hot sauce alongside for guests to add themselves.

Sides

Marmalade-roasted carrots *and* chickpeas *with* dates *and* feta

Carrots, apparently, are one of the most wasted foods. Save them – even the limper ones – by making this salad. It's glorious. I often serve this with barbecued butterflied lamb, roast chicken or whole baked fish. Or serve it as part of a mezze, with hummus, a salad (the tabouleh on page 129 would be wonderful) and some flatbreads for a light and satisfying lunch.

Leftovers: carrots

Serves 4
Preparation: 10 minutes
Cooking: 50 minutes

500g (1lb 2oz) carrots
2 Tbsp extra virgin olive oil, plus extra
   to serve
1 x 400g (14oz) can chickpeas
   (garbanzo beans), drained – save
   the liquid for another purpose
   (see the aquafaba chocolate mousse
   on page 162)
3 Tbsp marmalade
½ tsp dried thyme or mixed herbs
¼ tsp chilli flakes
4 dates, pitted and chopped
100g (about ¾ cup) crumbled feta
Fine sea salt
A squeeze of lemon, to serve

Preheat the oven to 190°C/170°C fan/375°F/Gas mark 5. Cut the carrots lengthways in half or quarters, so they are roughly the same size. Leave any very small carrots whole. Place in a large roasting tray, drizzle with the olive oil and sprinkle with salt. Roast for 30 minutes, or until almost tender.

Meanwhile, spread out the chickpeas (garbanzo beans) on paper towel and pat dry. Add to the tray with the carrots, shake to coat in the oil, and roast for a further 15 minutes.

Put the marmalade in a small pan with the dried herbs, chilli flakes and a pinch of salt. Gently warm, stirring, to loosen.

Pour the marmalade over the carrots and chickpeas and toss to combine. Return to the oven for a further 5 minutes.

Tip the carrots and chickpeas onto a serving platter and leave to cool slightly. Gently fold through the dates and feta. Drizzle with olive oil and squeeze over some lemon juice. Serve warm or at room temperature.

Try ...
Folding through a handful of very finely chopped parsley or carrot tops (if the carrots came with them attached).

Swap ...
Parsnips for the carrots – prepare in exactly the same way.

Roast potato salad *with* warm bacon, caper *and* chive dressing

Carbs doused in a sharp, salty, buttery dressing – it's very easy to eat a lot of this dish. I'm aware that in many households (mine included) the term 'leftover roast potatoes' is an oxymoron of sorts because there are rarely any roasties left after a roast dinner. However, I've taken to cooking extra (and hiding them) so we can enjoy this the next day with leftover cold meat and salad.

Leftovers: roast potatoes, scraps of bacon or ham

Serves 2–3
Preparation: 10 minutes

250g (9oz) roast potatoes, chopped
  into bite-sized pieces
2 Tbsp olive oil, plus a splash for
  frying the bacon or ham
2–3 smoked bacon rashers (strips) or
  40g (1½oz) leftover ham, chopped
1½ Tbsp sherry vinegar (red wine
  vinegar is fine)
30g (2 Tbsp) butter
1 garlic clove, finely chopped
1 heaped Tbsp capers, roughly
  chopped
2 Tbsp finely chopped chives
Mayonnaise, for drizzling

Have the potatoes ready in a serving bowl – you want them to be ready to accept the dressing while it's hot.

Warm a splash of olive oil in a frying pan (skillet) and add the bacon or ham. Fry over a medium heat until crisp at the edges. Scoop onto paper towel and set aside.

Add the vinegar to the same frying pan set over a medium heat. Scrape up any crispy bits with a wooden spoon while the vinegar bubbles. When reduced a little, add the olive oil, butter, garlic, capers and cooked bacon or ham. Stir everything together and let the mixture bubble gently for a minute or two.

Pour the hot dressing over the potatoes, add most of the chives and toss to combine. Drizzle over the mayonnaise, scatter over the remaining chives and serve immediately.

What about ...
Using cold boiled potatoes for this instead of roasties.

Freekeh *with* roast vegetables *and* maple dressing

This is very delicious, very quick and probably my favourite use of leftover roast veg. Use any kind, but it's particularly good with some root veg in the mix. The freekeh gives it bags of flavour, but it can be hard to find, in which case use another flavourful grain, such as spelt grain, pearl barley or wild rice.

Leftovers: cooked and uncooked vegetables

Serves 4
Preparation: 15 minutes
Cooking: 20 minutes

180g (generous 1 cup) freekeh
2 Tbsp sunflower seeds
300g (10½oz) roast vegetables, chopped into bite-sized pieces
A large handful of chopped soft herbs, such as parsley, coriander (cilantro), mint
Lemon juice, to taste

For the dressing
1 Tbsp maple syrup
1 Tbsp cider vinegar
4 Tbsp extra virgin olive oil
1 garlic clove, crushed or grated
¼ tsp ground cumin
Fine sea salt and freshly ground black pepper

Cook the freekeh according to the packet instructions.

Meanwhile, put all the dressing ingredients in a lidded jar, seal and shake to combine.

Toast the sunflower seeds in a dry frying pan (skillet) until golden and smelling fragrant.

When the freekeh is cooked, drain well and transfer to a platter. Pour over most of the dressing and toss to combine.

Add the vegetables, most of the seeds and herbs. Pour over the remaining dressing and gently toss. Scatter over the remaining seeds and herbs and serve immediately.

Crisper-drawer tabouleh *with* buckwheat *and* preserved lemon dressing

You can pretty much throw whatever fresh herbs and raw veg you like into this fresh and vibrant salad. It's bursting with flavour and terrific for using up big bunches or half-empty packets of fresh herbs. If any of them aren't exactly fresh and perky, soak in cold water first and dry well (ideally in a salad spinner) before slicing. The same applies to leafy greens, including lettuce.

I've offered a recipe below, but really go your own way. The key is to finely slice the herbs gently (don't chop or they go mushy). Chop your veg into tiny dice but grate broccoli and cauli using the large holes of a box grater.

The recipe yields about 12 heaped serving spoonfuls. If you aim for this quantity, you will have the right amount of dressing.

Leftovers: herbs, vegetables, mushrooms

Serves 4
Preparation: 15–20 minutes

1 x quantity preserved lemon dressing (see the lemon curd recipe on page 182)
3 Tbsp buckwheat
2 handfuls finely sliced mixed soft herbs (leaves and fine stalks), such as coriander (cilantro), parsley, dill, chervil, basil and tarragon*
A generous handful of finely sliced mint leaves
2 large button or chestnut mushrooms, finely chopped
1 large cauliflower floret, grated on the large holes of a box grater
2 medium ripe tomatoes, finely chopped, any juices reserved
1 celery stick or ½ courgette (zucchini), finely chopped
¼ large cucumber (about 80g/2¾oz), finely chopped
¼ red (bell) pepper, finely chopped
2 tsp baharat (see page 21)
Fine sea salt
Lemon juice, to serve

*don't use too much tarragon or dill as they are more pungent herbs

First make the preserved lemon dressing and set aside.

Toast the buckwheat in a dry frying pan (skillet) with a pinch of salt until it smells toasty. Set aside.

Place all the remaining ingredients except the lemon juice on a serving platter and season with salt. Add the toasted buckwheat and a generous pinch of salt, and gently toss to combine. Drizzle over half the dressing and toss to coat. Taste, and add more dressing or salt as needed. Serve at room temperature, within an hour or so, with a squeeze of lemon.

Try...
Using finely chopped toasted nuts – pistachios, walnuts or almonds – instead of buckwheat.

Saffron-roasted tomatoes *with* pistachios, herbs *and* salty cheese

This is a gorgeous dish if you have a glut of tomatoes or specimens that are woolly or unripe. Serve with roast meat or fish, part of a mezze or with the perfumed pasta and rice dish on page 132. It's also scrumptious stuffed into flatbreads, which will soak up the juices.

Leftovers: tomatoes

Serves 4
Preparation: 10 minutes
Cooking: 1½ hours

450g–600g (1lb–1lb 5oz) medium
   tomatoes, halved horizontally
Fine sea salt
¼ tsp caster (superfine) sugar
4 Tbsp olive oil
A pinch of saffron threads, finely
   chopped
A pinch of ground allspice
A pinch of ground coriander

To serve
1 Tbsp pistachios, toasted, roughly
   chopped
1 Tbsp chopped fresh tarragon or mint
   leaves, or more to taste
Crumbled or shaved salty cheese, such
   as ricotta salata, pecorino, feta or
   Parmesan

Preheat the oven to 180°C/160°C fan/350°F/Gas mark 4. Put the tomatoes cut-side up in a baking dish into which they fit snugly in a single layer (otherwise the juices will burn). Sprinkle generously with salt and the sugar.

Put the oil, saffron, allspice and coriander into a small pan and stir. Warm over a gentle heat until hot but not boiling. Spoon the fragrant oil over the tomatoes, including any strands of saffron. Roast for 1½ hours or until the tomatoes are very soft, slumping and slightly charred at the edges.

Remove the tomatoes from the oven and leave to cool a little (you want to eat them warm or at room temperature) then carefully transfer to a serving plate. Spoon over the juices, scatter over the pistachios and herbs and top with the cheese. Serve immediately.

Broken pasta *with* perfumed rice *and* mint butter

This fragrant side is versatile because it works so well with many different dishes, from stews to simple roast vegetables. It also utilizes all those annoying bits of pasta left in packets – including broken lasagne sheets.

Leftovers: broken pasta and pasta oddments

Serves 4 as a side
Preparation: 30 minutes
Cooking: 20 minutes

3 Tbsp vegetable oil
1 tsp ras el hanout
1 tsp ground turmeric
½ tsp ground cumin
A pinch of cayenne
2 large onions, halved and finely sliced
140g (5oz) uncooked pasta, any shape or a mix of shapes
40g (3 Tbsp) unsalted butter
140g (about ¾ cup) long-grain white rice
Fine sea salt

For the mint butter
40g (3 Tbsp) butter
1½ Tbsp dried mint

Warm the oil in a frying pan (skillet) over a medium heat and stir in the spices. Add the onions and a generous pinch of salt. Stir to coat in the spicy oil and gently fry until starting to soften, about 3 minutes. Add a splash of water, reduce the heat to low and cook until very soft, about 15 minutes, stirring now and then.

Meanwhile, if you're using up an array of different pasta sizes and shapes, pop them in a ziplock bag and lightly bash with a rolling pin to break them up a bit. Put the kettle on to boil at least 1 litre (4 cups) of water.

Melt the butter in a large saucepan. When foaming, add the broken pasta and the rice, and cook, stirring, to lightly toast for a minute or two. Pour in enough of the just-boiled water to cover by 5cm (2in) or so and add ¼ teaspoon of salt. Simmer for 10 minutes (top up with more just-boiled water if necessary). The rice might still be a little firm. Drain and then rinse under cold running water.

Remove half the onions from the frying pan and set aside. Add the drained pasta and rice to the pan with the remaining onions, stir, reduce the heat to low and cover. Cook for a further 10 minutes.

Meanwhile, to make the mint butter, melt the butter in a small pan and add the mint. Set the pan half-on the lowest heat to infuse and keep warm.

When the rice is done, taste and add more salt as needed – it's likely to need quite a bit. Tip onto a serving platter, top with the reserved onions and drizzle with the mint butter. Serve immediately.

Warm root veg *and* apple slaw with walnuts *and* dried cranberries

Use up odds and ends of root vegetables in this lovely warm spin on conventional coleslaw. Gentle cooking allows the vegetables to retain some soft crunch but they soak up more of the dressing than if they were raw. Don't be tempted to grate the veg or apple, as they will turn to mush. I use a mandoline to finely slice them, then I cut the slices into matchsticks. Sprinkle with a little lemon juice as you go to prevent browning, particularly the apple and celeriac (if using).

Leftovers: root vegetables, cabbage

Serves 4
Preparation: 20 minutes

1 apple
Lemon juice, for sprinkling
2 Tbsp olive oil
1 red onion, peeled, halved and finely sliced
¾–1 tsp caraway seeds (depending on your love of caraway)
150g (5½oz) root veg such as celeriac (celery root), parsnip or turnip (rutabaga), cut into fine matchsticks
1 medium carrot, cut into fine matchsticks
150g (5½oz) Savoy or sweetheart (Hispi) cabbage, finely sliced
40g (about ½ cup) roughly chopped walnuts, toasted
40g (about ½ cup) dried cranberries or cherries, chopped
Fine sea salt and freshly ground black pepper

For the dressing
100g (½ cup) Greek yoghurt
4 Tbsp good mayonnaise
2 Tbsp lemon juice
2 Tbsp olive oil
1 garlic clove, crushed

Start with the dressing. Put all the ingredients with salt and pepper to taste in a lidded jar, seal and shake to combine. Set aside.

Core the apple and cut into fine matchsticks. Transfer a bowl and sprinkle with lemon juice. Set aside.

Warm the olive oil in a large frying pan (skillet), add the onion and caraway seeds and gently stir-fry with a good pinch of salt for 2 minutes.

Add the root vegetables, including the carrot, and gently stir-fry with another pinch of salt for 2 minutes. Add the cabbage and gently stir-fry for 2 minutes more. The root veg should have softened but retain some bite.

Transfer the vegetables to a serving platter or bowl, add the apple and toss with the dressing. Taste, and add more seasoning if needed. Scatter over the walnuts and dried fruit and serve.

Chilli roast vegetables *with* toasted seeds *and* tahini yoghurt

Wrinkly radishes, limp parsnips, neglected heels of butternut squash, lonely Brussels sprouts from Christmas... cooked this way they segue from tired to tasty. Roasted seeds provide crunch and yoghurt gives delicious creaminess. There are a few components to pull together, but this dish delivers maximum flavour for relatively little effort. Terrific served with BBQ meat and flat bread.

Leftovers: uncooked odds and ends of vegetables

Serves 4
Preparation: 10 minutes
Cooking: 40 minutes

For the vegetables
40g (3 Tbsp) butter
50g (3 Tbsp) sweet chilli sauce
½ Tbsp olive oil
About 700g (1lb 9oz) uncooked veg, such as beetroot (beet), carrots, sweet potato, parsnips, celeriac (celery root), chopped into small pieces roughly the same size
Fine sea salt and freshly ground black pepper

For the seeds
2 Tbsp pumpkin seeds
2 Tbsp sunflower seeds
2 tsp za'atar (see page 96)
½ Tbsp olive oil
A generous pinch of fine sea salt and freshly ground black pepper

For the tahini yoghurt
200g (1 cup) Greek yoghurt
40g (scant ¼ cup) tahini, stirred well
1 tsp lemon juice, or more to taste
1 small garlic clove, grated

Preheat the oven to 180°C/160°C fan/350°F/Gas mark 4. For the vegetables, set a large toasting tray set over a medium heat on the hob and add the butter. When melted, stir in the sweet chilli sauce, olive oil and lots of salt and pepper. Stir well and cook until slightly reduced and sticky, then remove from the heat.

Add the vegetables to the tray and toss so everything is coated. Roast for 40 minutes, shaking the tray halfway through, or until the veg are tender (the exact time will depend on how small you have chopped the veg). Leave to cool a little.

Meanwhile, mix the seed ingredients together and spread out on a baking sheet lined with baking paper. Slide onto a rack below the tray of vegetables. If this isn't possible, just set the baking sheet on top of the roasting tray. Roast the seeds for 10–12 minutes until golden, then remove from the oven and set aside.

Mix the ingredients for the tahini yoghurt together with salt to taste and chill until needed.

To serve, spread the tahini yoghurt over a serving platter and top with the roast vegetables. Scatter over the toasted seeds. Serve immediately.

Try...
Sprinkling dukkah over the vegetables instead of the seed mix – you'll find the recipe on page 174.

Or...
Use almond or peanut butter instead of tahini mixed into the Greek yoghurt.

Sweet Things

Honeyed tutti frutti

Fruit gently imbued with honey and kissed with a hint of rosemary – I adore this method of preserving fruit. It's brilliant for using up stone fruit and pears that just won't ripen. I've also preserved a glut of apples, and tart raspberries and blackberries. This recipe is designed to extend the life of fruit by 2–3 weeks, perhaps a little more, but not for long-term storage. The tutti frutti is wonderful served with thick Greek yoghurt or ice cream, or alongside a slice of plainish cake for an easy dessert.

Leftovers: stone fruit, pears, apples or berries

Makes enough to fill a 500ml (17fl oz) jar
Preparation: 25 minutes

50g (¼ cup) caster (superfine) sugar
80g (¼ cup) floral honey
250ml (generous 1 cup) water
About 200g (7oz) fruit – any kind but not bruised or mouldy
1 Tbsp alcohol, such as sweet wine or brandy (optional)
1 rosemary sprig

Wash a 500ml (17fl oz) jar and lid with soapy water and rinse well. To sterilize, boil the lid for 10 minutes and leave the jar in an oven heated to 150°C/130°C fan/300°F/Gas mark 2 for 15 minutes.

Put the sugar, honey and water in a small pan, bring to a gentle simmer and cook until the sugar has dissolved. Set the pan half-on a very low heat so it stays hot.

Wash the fruit well, then stone or core as needed and cut into small chunks. There's no need to peel unless using fruit with tough skins, such as pineapple and kiwi. Pack the fruit into the hot sterilized jar and tuck in the rosemary sprig, leaving a good 5cm (2in) gap between the top of the fruit and the lid. Pour the hot honey syrup over the fruit – it should be completely covered. Add the alcohol (if using) and seal tightly.

Leave to cool, then store in the fridge. Ideally, leave the fruit for a week before eating, so the flavours infuse. The fruit should be fine for 2–3 weeks.

Sticky ginger cake

It's easy to make too much porridge (oatmeal) and easier still to chuck out what you don't eat – but that would be wrong. There are lots of lovely ways to use up leftover porridge (see page 181 for another option) but the best, in my opinion, is this divine sticky ginger cake. Of course, you don't have to make this as soon as you've finished breakfast. Leftover porridge will last in the fridge for a couple of days, and it freezes well – just defrost when you feel a sticky ginger cake urge coming on.

Leftovers: porridge, crystallized or preserved stem ginger

Preparation: 15 minutes
Cooking: 30 minutes

Vegetable oil, for brushing
175g (1⅓ cups) plain (all-purpose) flour
½ tsp ground cinnamon
1½ tsp ground ginger
¾ tsp bicarbonate of soda (baking soda)
A pinch of fine sea salt
80g (⅓ cup) unsalted butter
130g (about 6 Tbsp) golden syrup
130g (about 6 Tbsp) black treacle (molasses)
140g (about 1 cup) cold porridge (oatmeal)
1 large egg
25g (¼ cup) chopped crystallized ginger, roughly chopped

Preheat the oven to 180°C/160°C fan/350°F/Gas mark 4. Line a 20cm (8in) square baking dish with baking paper so it comes up and over the sides: lightly brushing the dish with oil first keeps the paper in place.

Put the flour, spices, bicarbonate of soda (baking soda) and salt in a mixing bowl and combine with a fork.

Melt the butter in a medium pan then remove from the heat. Stir in the syrup and treacle (molasses). Loosen the porridge (oatmeal) by stirring it well, then add to the buttery syrup along with the egg. Beat with a wooden spoon to thoroughly combine and break up larger bits of porridge.

Stir the mixture into the flour and spices, until everything is fully combined. Pour into the prepared dish, making sure the batter fills the corners. Smooth the top and stud with chopped ginger.

Bake for 30 minutes, or until firm to touch and an inserted skewer comes out clean. Leave in the dish for 10 minutes, then lift out onto a wire rack to cool using the overhanging baking paper as handles.

Root veg *and* poppy seed cake *with* orange buttercream

Dig out the root veg you've been neglecting – as well as pumpkin – and make a cake. This one is simple but moist and fragrant, and you would never know you're getting some of your five-a-day in every delicious slice.

Leftovers: root veg and/or pumpkin

Makes 1 x 23cm (9in) cake,
  serves 8–10
Preparation: 25 minutes
Cooking: 25 minutes

100ml (¼ cup plus 2 Tbsp) vegetable
  oil, plus extra for oiling
300g (2¼ cups) self-raising (self-
  rising) flour
1 tsp baking powder
1 tsp ground nutmeg
½ tsp cinnamon
3 Tbsp poppy seeds
½ tsp fine sea salt
3 large eggs
140g (scant ¾ cup) soft light
  brown sugar
3 Tbsp maple syrup
100ml (¼ cup plus 2 Tbsp) milk
2 tsp vanilla extract
150g (5½oz) root vegetables, such
  as carrots, parsnips and swede
  (rutabaga), or pumpkin, trimmed,
  peeled and grated

For the orange buttercream
100g (scant ½ cup) unsalted butter
200g (1½ cups) icing (confectioner's)
  sugar
Finely grated zest and juice of 1 small
  orange

Preheat the oven to 180°C/160°C fan/350°F/Gas mark 4. Oil a 23cm (9in) springform cake tin and line the base with baking paper.

Using a fork, combine the flour, baking powder, nutmeg, cinnamon, poppy seeds and salt in a mixing bowl.

In a separate bowl, beat the eggs and sugar together. Stir in the maple syrup, milk, vanilla and oil.

Stir the wet ingredients into the dry, making sure everything is well combined, then fold in the grated veg. Pour into the prepared tin and bake for 25 minutes, or until an inserted skewer comes out clean. Leave in the tin for 10 minutes then release and transfer to a wire rack to cool completely.

Meanwhile, beat the butter for the buttercream with electric beaters or by hand until pale and fluffy. Beat in the icing sugar, then the orange zest and salt. Gradually add enough of the orange juice to produce a soft and creamy icing that's loose enough to swirl over the cake but still holds its shape.

Spread the top of the cooled cake with the icing, swirling it if you like.

Fruity crème fraîche cake

Tender, damp and simple – this is my idea of a perfect cake, and it's super-flexible. I love using overripe bananas in the batter and studding the top with wrinkled grapes – they plump up deliciously in the oven and give an extra pop of juicy flavour. But see my suggestions below for other fruits that also work well.

Leftovers: overripe fruit like bananas, grapes and berries; crème fraîche or yoghurt

Serves 8–10
Preparation: 20 minutes
Cooking: 1 hour

100g (½ cup minus 1 Tbsp) unsalted butter, plus extra for greasing
100g (1 cup) ground almonds
100g (⅔ cup) fine semolina (farina)
1 Tbsp cornflour (cornstarch)
1½ tsp baking powder
A pinch of salt
2 large eggs, lightly beaten
100g (scant ½ cup) crème fraîche (Greek yoghurt also works)
2 black-skinned bananas, puréed (use a food processor or a fork)
2 Tbsp elderflower cordial (milk is fine too)
2 tsp vanilla extract or paste
100g (generous ½ cup) caster (superfine) sugar
A handful of grapes, wrinkled are great

Preheat the oven to 180°C/160°C fan/350°F/Gas mark 4. Grease a 20 x 10 x 7cm (4 cup) loaf tin (pan) and line the base and long sides with one piece of baking paper, so it hangs over the sides.

Put the ground almonds, semolina (farina), cornflour (cornstarch), baking powder and salt in a mixing bowl and combine using a fork. Set aside.

Put the eggs, crème fraîche, puréed bananas, cordial and vanilla in a jug and whisk together. Set aside.

In a separate bowl, beat the butter and sugar with hand-held electric beaters (or in a stand mixer) until pale and creamy.

Gradually beat the wet and dry ingredients into the butter and sugar mixture, alternating until everything is combined. Spoon into the prepared loaf tin, making sure the batter fills the corners. Lightly press the grapes into the top. Bake for 1 hour, or until a skewer inserted into the centre comes out clean. Leave in the tin for 10 minutes, then lift out onto a wire rack to cool, using the baking paper for handles.

Try ...
Using 1 large apple or pear, grated, instead of overripe bananas.

Topping with raspberries, blueberries or blackberries rather than the grapes. Poached fruit is also lovely on top – rhubarb is delicious.

Bread *and* jam steamed pudding

This was a revelation when I first made it. I couldn't believe bread could be transformed into something so delicious. A savoury Austrian dish known as 'napkin pudding' was my inspiration. It comprises a dough made from stale bread that's rolled up in a linen napkin, boiled, then sliced and served as an accompaniment to meat. (I've made this and served the slices fried: it's lovely.) This sweet version is a cross between a bread-and-butter pudding and a steamed pudding – it might not be a looker, but it tastes wonderful.

Leftovers: stale or surplus bread

Serves 6
Preparation: 15 minutes
Cooking: 1 hour 15 minutes–1 hour
*   30 minutes*

60g (¼ cup) unsalted butter, melted, plus extra for greasing
1 medium apple
Lemon juice, for sprinkling
200g (7oz) stale white bread, including crusts if they're not too hard
2 large eggs
70g (scant ½ cup) caster (superfine) sugar
100ml (1¼ cups plus 1 Tbsp) full-fat (whole) milk, plus extra if needed
2 tsp vanilla extract
1 tsp baking powder
A generous pinch of salt
140g (5oz) of your favourite jam (jelly)

Generously grease a 1 litre (4 cup) pudding basin (or one a bit larger). Cut out a circle of baking paper the size of the rim. Set aside.

Peel, core and chop the apple into small dice. Transfer to a mixing bowl as you go and toss with a little lemon juice to prevent browning. Set aside.

Put the bread and melted butter in the bowl of a food processor. Blitz to fine crumbs. Add all the remaining ingredients except the jam (jelly) and blitz to a smooth batter that drops easily off a spoon; you may need to add more milk. Pour the batter into the mixing bowl with the apple and stir to combine.

Stir the jam to loosen and spoon half into the bottom of the basin. Swirl the rest of the jam into the batter, then pour into the pudding basin. Smooth the top and cover with the circle of baking paper.

Lay a large piece of baking paper on top of a sheet of foil. Fold a pleat down the middle (so the pudding can expand) and place it, baking paper-side down, over the basin. Tie a length of string under the rim of the basin to secure the foil and paper. Thread another piece of string on either side to make a handle.

Boil in a double boiler for 1 hour 15 minutes, topping up with more boiling water if needed. To check if the pudding is ready, lift it out of the boiler and carefully remove the foil and paper. The top should be puffed and firm to touch but still sticky. If it's not quite ready, replace the paper circle, baking paper and foil and boil for a further 15 minutes, or until cooked.

Remove the basin from the pan and allow the pudding to rest for 10 minutes. Run a palette knife around the sides before turning out. Serve with cream or ice cream.

Try ...
Using a pear that needs using up instead of an apple.

Brown butter *and* cardamom rice pudding

Rice pudding is usually made with pudding rice, a starchy, round short-grain variety that yields an especially creamy texture. There were doubters in my household who said this couldn't be made successfully with cooked long-grain rice. They were wrong. The condensed milk provides the extra creaminess, and the result is fantastic.

Leftovers: cooked rice

Serves 4–6
Preparation: 15 minutes
Cooking: 1 hour 20 minutes

20g (1½ Tbsp) unsalted butter, plus
   extra for greasing
3 cardamom pods, crushed
300g (about 2¼ cups) cooked long-
   grain rice
A pinch of ground cinnamon
200g (¾ cup) condensed milk
400ml (1¾ cups) cream
200ml (¾ cup) milk
Finely grated zest of ½ lemon
A pinch of salt
Marmalade (or jam/jelly), to serve

Preheat the oven to 140°C/120°C fan/275°F/Gas mark 1 and grease a 25cm (10in) square baking dish.

Melt the butter in a small pan over a medium heat. When it foams, add the crushed cardamon pods and any seeds that have escaped. Cook until the butter is dark brown and smells nutty. Remove from the heat and leave to cool a little.

Put the remaining ingredients except the marmalade in a large jug then add the butter and cardamom pods, scraping in any caramelized bits from the bottom of the pan. Give everything a good stir to combine and break up any rice clumps.

Pour into the prepared dish and bake, uncovered, for 1 hour–1 hour 20 minutes, stirring every now and then. Remove from the oven when the top has set, and the pudding is the consistency you love. Serve immediately, with a spoonful of marmalade or jam (jelly).

Try ...
Adding a pinch of saffron or a bay leaf instead of (or as well as) cardamom. A good grating of nutmeg is a delicious alternative to cinnamon.

Cherry *and* vanilla rice tart

Cold cooked rice transformed! This is deeply delicious and reminiscent of a Bakewell tart. I love the contrast of the tangy dried cherries against the sweet vanilla-scented rice, although feel free to use up what you have in terms of dried fruit and jam (jelly). Be sure to make the rice filling just before the tart goes into the oven. If you make it first and let it sit for a while, the filling stiffens and the tart just won't be as moist and tender as it should be.

Leftovers: cooked rice

Serves 6–8
Makes 1 x 20cm (8in) tart
Preparation time: 10 minutes plus
*   30 minutes chilling*
Cooking time: 55 minutes

1 sheet ready-rolled shortcrust pastry
3 Tbsp cherry jam (jelly)
1 large egg, lightly beaten
250g (about 2 cups) cold cooked long-
    grain white rice
40g (¼ cup) caster (superfine) sugar
3 Tbsp milk, or more if needed
1 tsp baking powder
A pinch of salt
2 tsp vanilla extract or paste
30g (about 3 Tbsp) dried cherries,
    roughly chopped
40g (½ cup) flaked (slivered) almonds

Preheat the oven to 180°C/160°C fan/350°F/Gas mark 4 and slide a baking sheet inside.

Line a 20cm (8in) tart tin with the pastry (save the trimmings – see page 177), prick holes in the base with a fork and chill for 30 minutes. Line with baking paper and fill with baking beans (or use dried beans or rice). Transfer to the hot baking sheet and bake for 15 minutes. Remove the baking paper and beans and bake for a further 10–15 minutes, until pale gold. Remove from the oven and put the baking tray back in to stay hot.

Give the jam (jelly) a good stir to loosen and spread over the base of the pastry case.

Now make the filling. Put all the remaining ingredients except the cherries and almonds in the bowl of a food processor and whizz together. You want the mixture as smooth as possible and to drop easily off a spoon; add more milk if necessary. Stir in the dried cherries and immediately spoon the batter into the pastry case. Sprinkle over the almonds and bake for 20–25 minutes or until the filling is just set.

Serve warm with cold crème fraîche or softly whipped cream.

Try ...
Making pancakes with the fillling batter instead of a tart filling but leave out the dried fruit and nuts. Add heaped dessertspoonfuls to a hot frying pan (skillet) greased with butter. Cook for 1–2 minutes on each side until golden – they burn easily so don't have the heat too high. Serve with your favourite pancake toppings – fresh berries with yoghurt are lovely.

Honeyed wheaten bread *with* jumbled nuts, seeds *and* fruit

If your store cupboard (pantry) is littered with half-used packets of nuts, seeds and dried fruit, stop here. This loaf doesn't care if nuts are soft and past their prime, or whether you add particular seeds or dried fruit. Tumble in what's lurking in your store cupboard and you'll be rewarded with a highly moreish loaf that's heavenly spread thickly with good salty butter and/or golden syrup or served with cheese.

Leftovers: nuts, seeds, dried fruit

Serves 8–10
Preparation: 20 minutes
Cooking time: 45–50 minutes

60g (¼ cup) cold unsalted butter, cut into small cubes, plus extra for greasing
180g (scant 1½ cups) wholemeal (whole wheat) flour
180g (scant 1½ cups) plain (all-purpose) flour
30g (scant ¼ cup) porridge oats (rolled oats), plus extra for scattering on top
1 tsp bicarbonate of soda (baking soda)
¼ tsp fine sea salt
40g (1½oz) mixed nuts, lightly toasted and roughly chopped
40g (1½oz) mixed seeds
80g (2¾oz) mixed dried fruit, roughly chopped
60g (about ¼ cup) runny honey
250g (1¼ cups) Greek yoghurt, crème fraîche or soured cream (or a mixture)
5 Tbsp milk, or as much as needed

Preheat the oven to 180°C/160°C fan/350°F/Gas mark 4. Grease a loaf tin (loaf pan) roughly 23 x 13 x 7cm (8 cups) and line the long sides and base with one large sheet of baking paper that overhangs the sides.

In a large bowl, combine the flours, oats, bicarbonate of soda (baking soda) and salt by stirring with a fork. Rub the cubed butter into the flour mixture with your fingertips until it resembles breadcrumbs. Add the nuts, seeds and dried fruit and mix to evenly distribute – hands work best for this.

Mix the honey into the yoghurt, then stir into the dry mixture. Gradually add the milk, mixing with your hands between each addition, to make a sticky dough. Scrape the dough into the prepared tin and smooth the top with the back of a wet spoon, pushing it into the corners.

Scatter over a small handful of oats. Bake for 45–50 minutes, or until risen and golden, and a skewer inserted into the centre comes out clean. Leave in the tin for 10 minutes, then lift out onto a wire rack to cool, using the baking paper as handles.

Try ...
Using leftover porridge (oatmeal) instead of uncooked oats. Omit the 30g (scant ¼ cup) oats, reduce the yoghurt to 200g (1 cup) and stir in 60g (about ½ cup) cold porridge.

Salted cocoa, tahini *and* buckwheat crunch

This is the best way I know of to use up odds and ends of packets and nuts and seeds, especially those that have gone a little soft. It also makes delicious use of an egg white. The buckwheat isn't essential, but it adds a lovely depth of flavour and crunch. Enjoy as a rich chocolate-scented breakfast cereal or a crunchy topping for ice cream and/or cooked fruit.

Leftovers: egg white, odds and ends of stale nuts and seeds

Makes about 350g (12oz)
Preparation: 5 minutes
Cooking: 1 hour

3 Tbsp buckwheat (or mixed seeds)
100g (about ¾ cup) porridge oats
  (rolled oats)
60g (2¼oz) mixed seeds
60g (2¼oz) mixed nuts, roughly
  chopped (not too small)
40g (3¼ Tbsp) soft light brown sugar
15g (2 Tbsp) cocoa powder
A good pinch of fine sea salt
80g (¼ cup) honey
2 tsp tahini
2 tsp olive oil
1 egg white
A handful of dried fruit, chopped
  if large (optional)

Preheat the oven to 150°C/130°C fan/300°F/gas mark 2 and line a baking sheet with baking paper.

Put all the dry ingredients in a mixing bowl and stir well with a fork to distribute everything evenly.

Mix together the honey, tahini, oil and egg white. Pour into the nut mixture and stir to coat all the dry ingredients.

Spread the mixture out as thinly and evenly as possible on the prepared baking sheet – use the back of a dessertspoon. Bake for 30 minutes then remove from the oven and stir the mixture well, turning it over so the mixture at the bottom is at the top.

Bake for a further 30 minutes, turning again after 15 minutes.

Leave to cool on the baking sheet – it will crisp up nicely – then stir through the dried fruit. Store in an airtight container.

Hazelnut *and* orange flower meringue cookies

A cross between a meringue and a macaroon with a chewy cookie texture – these delicious hybrids are an excellent way to use up egg whites. They're not as tooth-achingly sweet as straight meringues, and they don't need the addition of whipped cream or fruit – just enjoy with a cup of strong coffee.

Leftovers: egg whites

Makes 18
Preparation: 15 minutes
Cooking: 1 hour

2 egg whites
115g (generous ½ cup) soft light brown sugar
⅛ tsp orange flower water
50g (½ cup) finely ground toasted hazelnuts (use a blender or spice grinder)

Preheat the oven to 140°C/120°C fan/275°F/Gas mark 1 and line a baking sheet with baking paper. Using hand-held electric beaters or a stand mixer, beat the egg whites until soft peaks form, then gradually beat in the sugar on low speed. Increase the speed until you have a thick and glossy meringue that doesn't fall off the beaters. Beat in the orange flower water then fold in the hazelnuts.

Scoop dessertspoonfuls of the mixture onto the prepared tray, spacing them 5cm (2in) apart. Flatten slightly with the back of a spoon. Bake for 1 hour and transfer to a wire rack to cool. Store in an airtight container.

Breakfast cereal gelato

Boxes of breakfast cereal rarely get fully eaten in our household, which I find baffling. So, I turned Weetabix remnants into gelato, which doesn't hang about for long. I've used a little honey as well as sugar in the mix, in homage to the way I devoured Weetabix as a kid. Cheerios also work well. Try offering a scoop to fellow ice-cream lovers without telling them what's in it and see if they can work it out.

Leftovers: breakfast cereal

Makes about 800ml (28fl oz)
Preparation: 15 minutes, plus overnight chilling, churning and freezing time

300ml (1¼ cups plus 1 Tbsp) full-fat (whole) milk
90g (½ cup) caster (superfine) sugar
40g (about 3 Tbsp) runny honey
3 Weetabix (about 60g/2¼ oz) or 100g (4 cups) cheerios
200ml (scant 1 cup) double (heavy) cream
Pinch of fine sea salt

Gently heat the milk, sugar and honey in a pan, stirring until everything is dissolved. Take the pan off the heat.

Break or pour the cereal into the pan and stir to completely combine with the liquid. Allow to cool a little, then blitz in a blender until completely smooth. Transfer to a jug, cover and chill overnight.

When you're ready to make the gelato, lightly whip the cream and fold into the cereal mixture.

If using an ice-cream maker, churn according to the manufacturer's instructions. If not, transfer to a shallow freezerproof container and freeze until frozen around the edges. Beat with hand-held electric beaters or whisk with a fork to break up the crystals, then return to the freezer. Repeat every 1½ hours or so until the mixture is frozen but has scoopable consistency. Take out of the freezer 10 minutes before serving.

What about ...
Swirling fruit purée through the churned gelato before putting it in the freezer.

Grapes in sweet wine *with* honeyed yoghurt cream

You buy bunches of perfect grapes that lounge beautifully in your fruit bowl like a still life, but before you know it, they're shrunken and wrinkly. The thing is, they're not ready for the bin. Here, heat and a splash of booze plump them up and intensify their flavour (grapes can, in truth, be a little sugary and bland) to make a fruity and jammy compote. I've deliberately made the servings small because it's deliciously rich.

Leftovers: grapes

Serves 2
Preparation: about 25 minutes

250g (9oz) grapes, wrinkled ones are fine but discard any that are mouldy
2 Tbsp caster (superfine) sugar
125ml (½ cup) sweet wine, such as a Sauternes, Moscatel, Moscato, or a sweet sherry
160g (¾ cup) Greek yoghurt
160ml (scant ¾ cup) double (heavy) cream
1 Tbsp runny honey
4 Biscoff biscuits, amaretti or ginger biscuits (gingersnaps), broken into pieces
40g (about ⅓ cup) blanched almonds, toasted and roughly chopped

Destem the grapes and put them in a small frying pan (skillet), sprinkle over the sugar and add a splash of water. Set the pan over a high heat and cook, shaking the pan, for 4–6 minutes, or until the grapes start to burst and release their juices. Add a splash more water if the pan starts to dry out.

Add the wine and let it bubble away over a medium heat for around 10 minutes, until the grapes have broken down and you have lots of syrupy juice. Remove the pan from the heat and allow to cool.

Combine the yoghurt, cream and honey in a mixing bowl and whisk to a soft dropping consistency.

Layer the yoghurt cream, grapes and syrup, biscuits and almonds in small glasses. Serve immediately.

Try ...
Using a layer of leftover cake – Christmas cake or pudding works well – between the fruit and the cream for a trifle-style pudding.

Coffee ground cookies

Most of us think of spent coffee grounds as a useless by-product of our daily brew – but these magical cookies prove otherwise. They're absolutely delicious, intensely flavourful and moreish. You can save the grounds until a cookie urge strikes. Just tip them into a ziplock bag and freeze, then defrost before use.

Leftovers: coffee grounds

Makes about 20
Preparation: 15 minutes plus 1 hour chilling
Cooking: 12 minutes

180g (1⅓ cups) plain (all-purpose) flour
40g (¼ cup) skinned hazelnuts, toasted and roughly chopped
50g (½ cup) cocoa powder
60g (2¼oz/10 tsp) spent coffee grounds
½ tsp bicarbonate of soda (baking soda)
A good pinch of fine sea salt
100g (scant ½ cup) softened butter
80g (scant ½ cup) soft light brown sugar
100g (generous ½ cup) caster (superfine) sugar
1 large egg, lightly beaten

Put the flour, nuts, cocoa powder, coffee grounds, bicarbonate of soda (baking soda) and salt in a medium bowl and stir well with a fork to combine.

Using a stand mixer or hand-held electric beaters, beat the butter and sugars together until pale and creamy. Gradually beat in the egg. Stir the dry ingredients into the butter mixture – it may seem too dry at first but keep mixing to make a stiff dough. Chill for at least 1 hour.

Preheat the oven to 180°C/160°C fan/350°F/Gas mark 4 and line a baking sheet with baking paper.

Pull off pieces of dough and roll into balls the size of large walnuts. Arrange on the prepared baking sheet about 7cm (2¾in) apart. If you need to bake in batches, keep the unused dough in the fridge. Bake for 6 minutes, then turn the baking sheet around and bake for 6 minutes more. As soon as the cookies come out of the oven, press down gently on each one with the bottom of a glass, just enough to flatten the top slightly. This results in a desirably chewy rather than cakey cookie.

Leave on the tray for a few minutes to firm up and then transfer to a wire rack to cool completely.

Try ...
Using different nuts in the cookies, such as almonds or pistachios.

Salted chocolate mousse *with* PX *and* maple glazed pecans

This dessert is virtually effortless and the best way to put the liquid from a can of chickpeas (garbanzo beans) – aquafaba – to good use. It might be useful to know that, just like egg whites, aquafaba freezes well. That means if you don't fancy making chocolate mousse in the same cooking session as the chickpeas, just freeze the liquid in an airtight container or ziplock bag and defrost before use. These servings are small because the mousse is incredibly rich.

Leftovers: aquafaba (chickpea/ garbanzo bean liquid)

Makes 4 small glasses
Preparation: 20 minutes

100g (3½oz) dark chocolate, 70% cocoa, broken into pieces
About 100ml (¼ cup plus 2 Tbsp) aquafaba, the liquid from a can of chickpeas (garbanzo beans)
1 Tbsp Pedro Ximénez (PX, an intensely sweet sherry)
40g (about ⅓ cup) pecans
4 Tbsp maple syrup
Sea salt flakes
Whipped cream or coconut cream, to serve (optional)

Put the chocolate in a heatproof bowl set over a pan of barely simmering water, being careful not to let the bottom of the pan touch the water. Stir now and then until melted. Remove the bowl from the pan and set aside to cool to room temperature.

Pour the aquafaba into a mixing bowl or the bowl of a stand mixer and whisk until very pale, fluffy and at least doubled in volume. This could take 8–10 minutes. Slowly add the PX by drizzling it down the side of the bowl so it doesn't force out any air. The mixture should be so stiff that it doesn't fall off the whisk or beaters.

Stir one-third of the aquafaba mixture into the cooled chocolate, then fold in the rest with a metal spoon. Try to lose as little air as possible from the aquafaba. Spoon into small glasses or ramekins and chill until ready to serve.

Meanwhile, lay a sheet of baking paper over a chopping board. Toast the pecans in a dry frying pan until they start to brown and smell toasty. With the pan over a medium-high heat, pour the maple syrup over the pecans and add a generous pinch of salt. Fry, stirring, until the pecans are sticky, and the maple syrup has reduced right down. Tip the pecans onto the baking paper and spread out to cool.

Serve the mousse sprinkled with sea salt flakes, pecans and a spoonful of cream for extra decadence.

What about ...
Swapping the Pedro Ximénez for bourbon, whisky, coffee liqueur or Cointreau and use almonds, hazelnuts or walnuts instead of pecans. You can also replace the maple syrup with honey.

Bits & Bobs

Crisper-drawer pickles

These are so good! Make them when you have a haul of oddments in the salad crisper drawer or a glut of vegetables you know you won't use up before they're past their best. The vegetables should be firm and in good nick – not too soft and without bruising. Save any softer, almost on-the-turn bits for the chutney on page 169.

You'll need to sterilize a jar – I used an old pickle jar with a 600ml (21fl oz) capacity, but you don't need one exactly the same size. Just make sure the vegetables are completely submerged in pickling liquid with at least 2cm (1in) 'headroom' between the top of the liquid and the lid.

Leftovers: vegetables that need using up

Makes enough to fill a 600ml (21fl oz) jar
Preparation: 30 minutes plus a couple of hours for salting and at least 2 weeks for the flavours to develop

450–500g (1lb–1lb 2oz) vegetables, such as celeriac (celery root), parsnip, swede (rutabaga), fennel, onion, carrot, broccoli and cauliflower (including their stalks), radishes, green beans, (bell) peppers, spring onions (scallions) – washed, peeled, trimmed and cut into 1.5cm (⅝in) pieces
15g (1 Tbsp) fine sea salt
250ml (generous 1 cup) apple cider vinegar (with at least 5% acetic acid)
125ml (½ cup) water
55g (¼ cup) caster (superfine) sugar
½ tsp mustard seeds
½ tsp fennel seeds
½ tsp coriander seeds
½ tsp black peppercorns
A pinch of ground turmeric
1 jalapeño chilli, sliced (optional)

Put all the vegetables into a bowl and sprinkle with the salt. Set aside for an hour or two. When the time is up, tip the vegetables into a colander (strainer) to drain.

Meanwhile, wash the jar and lid with soapy water and rinse well. To sterilize, boil the lid for 10 minutes and leave the jar in the oven at 150°C/130°C fan/300°F/Gas mark 2 for 15 minutes.

Put the remaining ingredients except the jalapeño in a small pan and bring to a simmer. Once the sugar has dissolved, set the pan half-on the lowest heat to keep the liquid hot but not bubbling.

Pack the vegetables into the hot sterilized jar, pouring over some of the pickling liquid between additions – include some of the aromatics as you want them distributed throughout the jar. Add the jalapeño (if using). Press down to ensure the veg are submerged, allowing the necessary 2cm (1in) 'headroom'. Secure the lid.

Opinion is divided over whether you need to heat-treat the pickled veg to prevent the growth of nasty bacteria. If you're only making one jar, and plan to eat the pickles once their flavours have had time to develop (at least 2 weeks) just store the jar in the fridge. If you're making more than this amount and/or would like a longer shelf life, follow the next step.

Place a folded tea towel (dish towel) in the bottom of a deep pan (this is to stop the glass rattling). Place the sealed jar(s) on the towel and pour in enough water to come three-quarters of the way up the sides. Bring to the boil over a medium heat and boil for 20 minutes. Carefully remove from the water and leave out to cool. If preserved correctly, they should keep well for months stored in a cool, dark place.

Fruit salad *and* lime jam

Overripe fruit has a superb future in the form of jam (jelly). This chunky version is completely flexible – you can mostly use whatever the fruit bowl has to offer. Because the recipe is for such a small batch, you don't have to heat-treat the jars, as I've assumed you'll eat it within a couple of weeks. (If you want to store it unopened for longer, heat-treat the jam using the method for Crisper-drawer pickles on page 167.) This recipe is perfect for stone fruit, berries or pears, although apples are not ideal as they take longer than the other fruit to soften.

Leftovers: fruit you need to use up

Makes 1 x 250ml (9fl oz) jar
Preparation: about 1 hour

500g (1lb 2oz) fruit, such as unpeeled peaches, plums, nectarines or pears (stoned or cored and chopped into 2cm/1in chunks), and also grapes or berries
200g (generous 1 cup) caster (superfine) sugar
Finely grated zest and juice of 1 lime

Thoroughly wash and dry a 250ml (9oz) jar and lid. Place a couple of small plates or ramekins in the freezer to test for a setting point.

Put the prepared fruit in a heavy pan with 250ml (generous 1 cup) of water. Simmer gently for 25–30 minutes until the fruit is soft and starting to collapse. Don't cook too rapidly or the liquid will cook off before the fruit has softened.

Stir in the sugar, the lime zest and juice. Heat gently until the sugar has dissolved.

Increase the heat and boil for about 15 minutes or until it reaches setting point – only stir now and again to stop it catching. Start testing for setting point when the jam (jelly) has begun to thicken and darken.

To test for setting point, remove the pan from the heat and take your plate from the freezer. Spoon a small blob of jam onto the plate and push it with your finger – if it wrinkles, it's ready. If not, continue cooking, testing for setting point every 3 minutes.

Spoon the hot jam into the jar and seal – it will keep well in the fridge for a couple of weeks.

Try...
Adding a few buds of lavender to the fruit when simmering instead of lime zest (use with restraint or the jam might end up overly perfumed). Or add ½ tsp mixed spice with the sugar (omit the lime) for jam that tastes a little bit of Christmas.

Rich fruit *and* vegetable chutney

Include any kind of surplus fruit and vegetable in this intense and richly spiced chutney, especially very soft, overripe or bruised specimens. Although it takes some time, it couldn't be simpler to make – most of what you have to do is stir the pot now and then. It's perfect to have on hand at Christmas – serve with the cheeseboard and/or ham – but wonderful any time of year slathered on cold meat sandwiches. Based on a recipe in *The Ethicurean Cookbook*.

Leftovers: surplus fruit and vegetables, especially bruised or overripe

Makes about 1kg (2lb 3oz)
Preparation: about 1 hour
*   20 minutes*

500g (1lb 2oz) mixed fruit and
   vegetables, such as pears, apples,
   stone fruit, sweet potato, pumpkin,
   turnips, parsnips, swede (rutabaga)
   and celeriac (celery root) – peeled,
   cored or stoned where necessary,
   and chopped small
400ml (1¾ cups) apple cider vinegar
500g (2½ cups) soft light brown sugar
300g (10½oz) dried fruit, such as
   apricots, figs, sour cherries,
   cranberries, dates and prunes
   (make sure they are pitted)
150g (about 1½ cups) finely chopped
   onion
4 garlic cloves
30g (2 Tbsp) fine sea salt
3 tsp mustard seeds
2 Tbsp ground ginger
1 scant tsp nigella seeds
½ tsp ground cinnamon
2 cloves

Put the fruit and vegetables in a large heavy pan with the vinegar and sugar. Bring to the boil and then reduce the heat and simmer very gently until the fruit and vegetables are soft and starting to break down.

Add all the remaining ingredients and simmer gently until thickened, about 40 minutes, stirring regularly.

Ladle into hot sterilized jars (see page 138 for how to sterilize your jars). Store in a cool, dark place. They will keep for about 6 months.

Whipped flavoured butter

As I write this, flavoured butter – also known as compound butter – is having a moment. Social media is gleaming with smooth quenelles of butter imbued with everything from miso paste or curry powder to herbs or Bloody Mary. It's easy to understand why; butter is a flavour carrier, so a scoop or disc served on top of meat, fish or vegetables can seriously ramp up the flavour of an otherwise plain dish.

For those who love finding nifty uses for leftovers, flavoured butters are a blessing. A spoonful of curry paste left in the jar, a bunch of herbs you won't use up before they wither, a tablespoon or two of capers, the remnants of a jar of honey that has crystallized… almost anything can be whipped into flavoured butter. These are quick and easy to make – it's just combining softened butter and something delicious into a tasty union. The added bonus is that they can be chilled or frozen to use later; so often we throw out leftovers simply because we can't use them immediately. I've suggested four flavoured butters here that make great use of leftovers, but the possibilities really are endless.

Leftovers: capers, fresh herbs, harissa paste, honey

Lemon caper butter
1 Tbsp finely chopped capers, rinsed
    if packed in salt
1 garlic clove, grated
1 Tbsp finely grated lemon zest
1 heaped Tbsp finely chopped parsley
½ tsp sea salt flakes

Garlic herb butter
2 Tbsp finely chopped herbs
¼ tsp freshly ground black
    peppercorns
1 garlic clove, grated
½ tsp sea salt flakes

Harissa and lime butter
1½ Tbsp harissa paste
Finely grated zest of 1 lime
½ tsp sea salt flakes

Vanilla bean and honey butter
2 Tbsp honey
½ Tbsp icing (confectioner's) sugar
½ tsp vanilla paste
A pinch of fine sea salt

For each, whip 100g (scant ½ cup) of unsalted butter until soft and creamy – use electric beaters for extra airiness – or simply mash with a fork. Then, beat in the ingredients listed.

Spoon the butter onto a rectangle of baking paper and roll into a cylinder, twisting the ends like a cracker. Chill, or if you want to freeze the butter, slice the cylinder into discs before wrapping. Then, just snap off one or two as needed.

Lemon caper butter
Place a disc on top of cooked chicken or seafood, or melt the butter and spoon over.

Garlic herb butter
A great all-rounder. Use for making garlic bread or serve with veg, meat, poultry or seafood.

Harissa and lime butter
Great with pork, lamb or beef.

Vanilla bean and honey butter
Slather on toast, muffins, crumpets or pancakes.

Seedy crackers

Once I've made a batch of these, I need to keep them at arm's length. Not only are they a brilliant and easy way to use up stale bread, they're also super moreish spread with butter, nut butter, hummus or dip. In all honesty, they're a much tastier cracker to serve with cheese than many of the expensive kinds you buy in a box.

Leftovers: bread, odds and ends of seeds

Preparation: 10 minutes plus
* 15 minutes soaking*
Cooking: 25–30 minutes

120g (4¼oz) leftover bread, including
  crusts, torn into small pieces
1 Tbsp runny honey
½ tsp fine sea salt
1 tsp olive oil
60g (2¼oz) mixed seeds (pumpkin,
  sunflower, sesame, quinoa, linseed,
  black sesame – make sure there are
  some larger ones in the mix)
Flaky sea salt, for sprinkling

Put the bread in a mixing bowl and sprinkle with just enough water to moisten, turning as you go to dampen it all. Set aside to soak for 15 minutes.

Once the bread has soaked, preheat the oven to 150°C/130°C fan/300°F/Gas mark 2. Transfer the bread to a food processor along with the honey, salt and oil. Blitz to a mixture that looks crumbly but sticks together when squeezed between your fingers. If too dry to do this, add a splash more water and blitz again.

Return the mixture to the mixing bowl and add the seeds. Mix and squeeze with your hands until the seeds are distributed and the mixture holds together like dough. Again, if a bit dry, add a splash more water.

Shape into a ball and flatten into a disc. Place between two large sheets of baking paper and roll out evenly, working outwards from the centre. You want the 'dough' to be extremely thin, barely a couple of millimetres.

Carefully peel back the top sheet of baking paper. Sprinkle over some sea salt flakes and cover again with the baking paper. Lightly roll to gently press in the salt. Peel off the top sheet of paper.

Carefully slide the seedy dough, on its baking paper, onto a baking sheet. Bake for 30 minutes or until dry in the centre and very lightly browned. Slide onto a wire rack – it will crisp up as it cools. Break into pieces and store in an airtight container.

For extra flavour try ...
Sprinkling garlic granules over the crackers before they go into the oven, or adding ½ tsp smoked paprika to the food processor when you blitz the dough.

Dukkah

Past-their-best nuts are often soft, waxy and unappealing – but can be revived in a hot pan and put to good use in this sublime Middle Eastern mix. It provides texture and incredible flavour to so many dishes, from eggs and salads to roast vegetables and breadcrumbs for chicken and fish. You can also enjoy dukkah the authentic way, mixed with olive oil to use as a dip for bread. The sweet version adds soft crunch when sprinkled on yoghurt, porridge (oatmeal), fruit salad, baked fruit, folded through softly whipped cream, or scattered over toast spread with nut butter.

Leftovers: odds and ends of nuts and seeds (including stale ones, but if the nuts smell or taste sour or nasty, they're probably rancid, so discard them)

Makes enough for 1 small jar
Preparation: 10 minutes

Savoury dukkah
60g (2¼oz) mixed nuts
4 Tbsp sesame seeds
2 Tbsp coriander seeds
2 Tbsp cumin seeds
1 tsp fennel seeds
1 tsp black peppercorns
2 tsp dried thyme
1 tsp sweet paprika
1 tsp fine sea salt

Sweet dukkah
60g (2¼oz) mixed nuts
1 Tbsp honey
40g (1½oz) mixed seeds (pumpkin, sunflower, sesame, quinoa, linseed, black sesame)
¾ tsp fennel seeds
A generous pinch of ground cumin
A generous pinch of ground coriander
1 tsp ground cinnamon
1 tsp caster (superfine) sugar
A pinch of sea salt flakes

Savoury dukkah
Heat the nuts in a dry frying pan (skillet) over a medium-high heat for 4–6 minutes, shaking frequently, until golden and fragrant. Tip into the bowl of a food processor.

Return the pan to the heat and add the seeds and peppercorns. Toast for 3 minutes, then transfer to the food processor. Add the thyme, paprika and salt, and briefly pulse to make a rough rubble. Store in an airtight container for up to 3 months.

Sweet dukkah
Heat the nuts in a dry frying pan (skillet) over a medium-high heat for 4–6 minutes, shaking frequently, until golden and fragrant. Reduce the heat to low, add the honey and stir to coat. Fry for 30 seconds or so, then tip out onto a sheet of baking paper. Spread out and leave to cool.

Wipe out the pan, return to a medium-high heat and lightly toast the mixed seeds and fennel seeds for 3 minutes.

When the nuts are completely cool, transfer to a food processor with the seeds, spices, sugar and salt. Pulse to make a rough rubble. Store in an airtight container for up to 3 months.

Bananascotch sauce

Black-skinned, ripe bananas are gold – and not just in banana bread. This moreish sauce is very easy to make and a good way to use up the end of a pot of cream. Pour over ice cream, plain cake or fruit salad (oh yes!). Or simply stand at the stove eating it straight from the pan (once it's cooled down enough, of course), congratulating yourself for not chucking out those bananas.

Leftovers: overripe bananas

Makes about 350ml (12fl oz)
Preparation: 15 minutes

250g (scant 1½ cups) caster (superfine) sugar
60ml (4 Tbsp) golden syrup
1 large ripe banana, puréed in a food processor
150ml (scant ¾ cup) double (heavy) cream
40g (3 Tbsp) unsalted butter
1 tsp vanilla extract
A generous pinch of sea salt flakes

Put the sugar, syrup and 4 Tbsp water in a heavy pan and stir together. Cook over a medium heat until the sugar has dissolved and the mixture is pale gold. Don't stir.

Increase the heat and let the mixture bubble but not boil wildly, swirling the pan now and then but not stirring, until it turns a rich amber colour, about 6 minutes. Be careful not to let it burn.

Take the pan off the heat and stir in the puréed banana – the mixture will splutter, so take care. Then stir in the cream, butter and vanilla.

If the caramel is too thin, return to the heat and simmer, stirring constantly, until it's voluptuously saucy. When done, add sea salt flakes to taste.

Try ...
Overripe or ripe bananas are terrific in cake (see recipe on page 144) and smoothies, or mashed up and stirred into pancake batter – but there are other uses. A classic one is to make a slit along the length of the unpeeled banana, slot in some chopped chocolate and wrap the whole thing in foil. Bake at 200°C/180°C fan/400°F/Gas mark 6 for about 20 minutes.

Sweet or savoury croustillants

Don't throw away leftover scraps of puff pastry! Those tart and pie trimmings can be transformed into delicious things. Here are a couple of ideas.

Leftovers: pastry

Spiced cocoa and fennel croustillants

For every 50g (1¾oz) of puff pastry scraps, combine: 3 tsp caster (superfine) sugar and 1 tsp ground cinnamon and/or cocoa powder with a tiny pinch of crushed fennel seeds and a tiny pinch of fine sea salt.

Preheat the oven to 200°C/180°C fan/400°F/Gas mark 6. Knead the pastry scraps together to amalgamate and roll out very thinly between two sheets of baking paper. Carefully peel off the top sheet and sprinkle the pastry with the sugary mixture – it will be generously coated. Slide the pastry, on its baking paper, onto a baking sheet and bake for 8 minutes or until golden underneath.

Cool on a wire rack and break into shards to serve.

Anchovy and cheese puffs

Weigh your pastry scraps and make a note of them. Knead the scraps together to amalgamate and roll out very thinly between two sheets of baking paper into a rectangle. Carefully peel off the top sheet and slide the pastry, on its baking paper, onto a chopping board.

For every 140g (5oz) of pastry, finely chop 10 anchovy fillets in oil (drained) and finely grate 25g (1oz) Parmesan. Scatter the anchovies and cheese over the pastry. Roll from one long side into a tight sausage shape then cut it crossways into 2cm (1in) slices. Arrange, cut-side up, on a baking sheet lined with the sheet of baking paper and brush the tops with beaten egg. Bake at 200°C/180°C fan/400°F/Gas mark 6 for 15–20 minutes or until puffed and golden.

Alternatively, freeze the puffs before baking. Transfer the slices to a small baking sheet or board and freeze. Once frozen, tip into a ziplock bag and bake from frozen, until cooked through completely, puffed and golden.

End of jar, bottle, pot and can ideas

The ideas on this page exemplify my mother's approach to food, and that of generations of home cooks before her; nothing should be wasted, not even the very last bits in jars, bottles and cans. Whether there's a spoonful left in the bottom or a scraping clinging to the sides, that's flavour, and it can all be put to good use.

If there's just a scraping ...

... of jam (jelly), honey, marmalade, Marmite, mustard, chilli paste, ketchup, brown sauce, chutney, pomegranate molasses, tamarind sauce, hoisin sauce, curry paste, miso paste (and, for that matter, a just-emptied can of tomatoes)

Add a little water, wine or vinegar. Replace the lid and shake well, then use this flavour essence to deglaze a pan or drizzle into stews and gravies to give them a boost.

... of mayonnaise, soured cream, cream, crème fraîche or yoghurt

Use this when making a vinaigrette or dressing to add a subtly creamy note. Add the lemon juice or vinegar component of the vinaigrette to your near-empty jar, cover and shake (or swirl the pot and tip into a jar). Add the remaining vinaigrette ingredients to the jar and shake again. Use the same approach with near-empty jars of nut butter, tahini and satay sauce.

If there are two or three spoonfuls left ...

... in a jar of nut butter

Add lime juice or rice vinegar, sweet chilli sauce, curry powder, soy sauce and a good splash of coconut milk. Cover and shake well. Taste and add more of any of the components you feel it needs. Serve with skewers of lamb or chicken or stirred through noodles.

... in a jar of lemon curd, honey, marmalade or jam

Add a good splash of olive oil, some dried mixed herbs, a couple of grated garlic cloves and lots of salt and pepper. Shake well. Rub over chicken thighs, pumpkin wedges or root vegetables and roast at 180°C/160°C fan/350°F/Gas mark 4 until cooked through.

... in a jar of pickled vegetables, cornichons or capers

Chop very finely and add to salads, dressings and sauces to brighten and add tang. Fold through yoghurt, crème fraîche or mayonnaise for a cheat's tartare sauce; also add a finely chopped shallot, lemon juice and chopped fresh herbs.

... of brine in a jar of pickled vegetables, cornichons, capers or preserved lemons

Use it to replace some of the vinegar or lemon juice component in vinaigrette. Or use as you would lemon juice to brighten stews, curries and sauces. Spoon a little over fried things – fritters, fish and chicken – to add zing and cut through the oiliness. Add a splash to a Martini. Sprinkle over potato salad. Add to bread dough instead of water. The brine from a packet of feta cheese can be used in the same way.

... of oil in a jar or can of sardines or anchovies

Use it to cook with or in dressings, as it's packed with savoury fishy flavour. Use to fry breadcrumbs for scattering over gratins or to toss through pasta; to fry off leafy greens, such as spinach, chard or kale; to sweat onions, carrots and celery when preparing the base of stews and sauces.

To use up leftover...

Here are some extra ideas to use up, or make the most of, leftover bits and bobs.

Cooked pasta with sauce

Stuff a scoop of spaghetti bolognaise, carbonara, macaroni cheese or any type of saucy pasta into a sandwich or toastie.

Curry sauce

Add to bubble and squeak or hash (see page 31) or to the mix for a stew or pie (see pages 16–21).

Lettuce and salad leaves

Treat as leafy vegetables in stir-fries, risotto and soups, or wilt in butter for a simple side dish – with or without peas, onion and bacon as per the French classic *petits pois à la française*.

Uncooked sausages

1. Fry, chop and add to the pasta bake, risotto, soup, stew, pie, hash or salad (see Master Recipes on pages 12–39).

2. Stir into this speedy pasta sauce: Fry 1 chopped onion in oil with a pinch of salt until soft and translucent. Add a chopped garlic clove, a pinch of fennel seeds and a pinch of chilli flakes. Cook for 2 minutes more. Add a squirt of tomato purée (paste) and a 400g (14oz) can chopped tomatoes. Season generously and simmer for 10–15 minutes, adding stock or water to loosen if necessary. Finish with a splash of cream, soured cream or crème fraîche if you have any to use up.

Risotto

Turn it into soup. Combine with enough good stock to make a soupy consistency and simmer gently until piping hot. Bulk out with chopped veg like red (bell) peppers, tomatoes, mushrooms or frozen peas. Add lemon juice and chopped fresh herbs to brighten.

Breadcrumbs

Whiz up stale bread in a food processor - lightly toast first if the bread is fresh and you know you won't use it up. Freeze in an airtight container or bag and use in the following ways:

1. Use to bind fishcakes and burgers or add to your favourite crumble mix.

2. Fry in olive oil with garlic and chilli flakes for a crispy pasta topping.

3. Make a crispy coating for fish or a flattened chicken fillet before frying: dip in flour first, then egg, then breadcrumbs.

4. Mix with salt and pepper, a splash of olive oil and finely grated Parmesan as a topping for gratins, pasta bakes and macaroni cheese.

Mashed potato

1. Thicken and enrich soups and stews. Loosen with a spoonful or two of stock or milk first, then stir into the cooking pot.

2. If you have lots of mash, make potato soup. Stir in enough hot stock to make a soup consistency, top with grated cheese, crispy onions or croûtons.

3. Add to bubble and squeak (see page 31), stuff into sandwiches with a pinch of curry powder, cold roast meat or vegetables and mango pickle, or slather on toast with some hot sauce and a fried egg.

Porridge

Add a few spoonfuls to your favourite pancake mixture with a splash of milk to loosen if too thick.

Herbs

1. Make a use-on-everything green sauce. Whizz a handful of surplus herbs (leaves and tender stalks) in a blender with the following: salad leaves and/or spring onions (scallions), lemon juice, olive oil, garlic and/or chilli flakes, soured cream or crème fraîche. Use as a dip (especially good made with soured cream) or drizzle into or over soups, stews, roast veg, roast meat, fish, salads or in sandwiches.

2. Make scented sugar. Blitz a small handful of tender leaves (basil and mint are delicious) with 100g (generous ½ cup) caster (superfine) sugar. Sprinkle over sliced fruit, stir into tea, or fold into gently whipped cream. Sugar flavoured with woody herbs, such as rosemary and thyme, is perfect for baking.

3. Make tartines. Finely chop the leaves and tender stems of any fresh herbs. Sprinkle over hot toast spread with goat's cheese, cream cheese or labneh. Shower with seeds, lots of salt and pepper and drizzle with good extra virgin olive oil.

Egg yolks

1. Make mayonnaise or whisk into vinaigrette/salad dressing for extra creaminess.

2. Beat into mashed potato, porridge, risotto or custard to add richness or mix with a splash of milk or water to glaze a pastry case before baking it.

3. Use to make a batch of shortcrust pastry, roll into a disc, wrap in a double layer of cling film (plastic wrap) and freeze until you want to make a tart or pie.

Egg whites

1. Make a fluffier-than-standard omelette or frittata by adding 1–2 extra whites per whole egg.

2. Brush over the base of a pastry case for the final part of blind baking (once you have removed the paper and baking beans) to seal and prevent a soggy bottom.

3. Make meringues or a light and fluffy angel food cake.

Cooked chicken

Add it to a zingy toastie. Use the toastie technique for the takeaway curry toastie on page 52 but fill the sandwich with shredded chicken, cheese and kimchee, sauerkraut or chopped pickles.

Preserved lemons

Make lemon curd. Halve and discard the seeds from 3 preserved lemons (about 120g/4½ oz), then remove most of the pulp. Put the rinds in a blender with the finely grated zest and juice of 1 lemon, 2 large eggs plus 2 egg yolks, and 120g (generous ½ cup) caster (superfine) sugar. Pour the mixture into a heatproof bowl set over a pan of barely simmering water. Whisk continuously for 5 minutes or so until the mixture heats up and thickens slightly. Add the butter bit by bit, whisking until it melts before adding the next bit, until all the butter is incorporated. Continue whisking until the curd is thick and ribbons from the whisk briefly hold their shape. Push the curd through a sieve, being sure to scrape the bottom. Set aside to cool. Store in a sealed jar in the fridge for up to two weeks.

1. Make a briny tangy vinaigrette using the preserved lemon pulp left over from the curd (above). Put 2 Tbsp of the finely chopped pulp into a lidded jar with 4 Tbsp extra virgin olive oil, 1½ Tbsp honey, 1½ Tbsp lemon juice or cider vinegar, 1 tsp Dijon mustard and some freshly ground black pepper. Shake well.

Roast beef

Make an aromatic chilli beef soup – this is enough for 2 people. Pour 500ml (17fl oz) beef stock (made with stock (bouillon) cubes is fine) into a pan and add 2 finely chopped spring onions (scallions), 1 tsp finely grated ginger, ½ cinnamon stick and ½ star anise. Heat gently, then add sriracha or your favourite chilli sauce to taste. Use this broth to cook 120g (4¼oz) egg noodles following the packet instructions, then add thinly sliced roast beef.

Dried fruit

Make no-cook energy balls. Blitz whatever dried fruit needs using up in a food processor with enough oats, nuts, seeds, a spoonful or two of peanut butter and a touch of cocoa powder (optional) to make a thick paste. Roll into balls with damp hands and store in the fridge.

Milk, cream, soured cream or crème fraiche

1. Add to cakes, pancakes and scones for extra tenderness.

2. Use milk to marinate meat and poultry to make it beautifully tender. Pop the dairy and meat in a container or plastic bag, along with any herbs or spices you fancy. Cover and leave in the refrigerator for up to 24 hours before cooking.

Tips

1. **Dairy products** often last longer than their best-by-date so have a sniff; if your milk or cream smells OK, it should be fine. Don't store either in the fridge door, which is the warmest part – instead, keep on a shelf.

2. To freeze **egg yolks**, whisk with a pinch of salt or sugar per yolk (depending on whether you will use them in sweet or savoury dishes) – this prevents thickening when defrosted. Freeze in a scrupulously clean, labelled airtight container. Egg whites just need to be frozen in an airtight container or bag.

3. To freeze leftover **rice**, make sure you cool the rice quickly (plunge the bowl or pan in a sink of cold water to speed up the process) and freeze in an airtight container within an hour of cooking. Defrost in the fridge and make sure you reheat the rice until piping hot.

4. Collect the **fat** from your roasts and pour into a jar for dripping and store in the fridge until needed. Or trim the fat from roast meat and render down in the frying pan for frying your bubble and squeak or hash.

5. To freeze **herbs**, finely chop and pack into ice cube trays leaving a little space at the top. Cover with olive oil. Once frozen, release them from the trays and store in airtight containers and bags. Defrost and add to dressings or sauces, or pop straight from frozen into the cooking pot.

6. In most recipes, soft **herbs** such as basil, parsley or coriander (cilantro) can be used interchangeably without impacting the flavour of a dish much, so use up what you have. (Some people aren't fond of dill, so use judiciously.) Woody herbs like rosemary and thyme can be swapped around, too.

How long do leftovers keep in the fridge and freezer?

Cooked leftover food should be cooled as quickly as possible and refrigerated within an hour of cooking and not left at room temperature Store in an airtight container or zip-lock bag.

'General' includes cooked vegetables, pasta and pasta sauces, cheese sauces, desserts, meat, poultry and seafood but **NOT** cooked rice.

Store rice in the fridge for no more than 1 day until reheating. Make sure rice goes in the freezer within 1 hour of cooking. Defrost it in the fridge and then reheat it until it is steaming hot before eating immediately. Rice can be frozen for up to 3 months.

	Fridge	Freezer
General cooked leftovers including meat, poultry and seafood	3–4 days	2–3 months
Raw minced meat and offal, including sausages	2–3 days	3–4 months
Raw beef, veal, lamb and pork	3–5 days	4–6 months
Raw egg whites*	Up to 4 days	Up to 1 year
Raw egg yolks*	Up to 4 days	Up to 1 year

*American Egg Board

Sources: US Department of Agriculture (USDA) and the Australian Commonwealth Scientific and Industrial Research Organisation (CSIRO).

Leftovers Index

Recipe Index

About the author

Sue Quinn is an award-winning food writer, cookbook author and journalist. Her articles and recipes regularly appear in the UK's leading food publications including the *Telegraph, Sunday Times, Guardian, Delicious, Waitrose* magazine and *BBC Food*. She has won the Fortnum & Mason's Online Food Writer Award and the Guild of Food Writer's award for her work on British food, and been shortlisted for the Guild of Food Writer's 2023 Food Writer's Award. *Second Helpings* is her 15th book.

Acknowledgements

I'm profoundly grateful to my family, Adam, Ruby and Ben, for their support and enthusiasm, constants that buoyed me up throughout this book's journey. I'm indebted to Ruby for her brilliant and efficient recipe testing, and to Adam and Ben for cheerfully dashing to the shops to replenish supplies whenever necessary. This book wouldn't have been possible without you all.

Thanks to Claire Apsden for enthusiastically accepting the results of my recipe testing. Also to Vanessa, Sam, Claire and the gang for all your positive comments, support and cake-eating skills. Diana Henry, I'm grateful as ever for your invaluable advice and encouragement, and to Catherine Phipps for saying the right thing when it was needed.

Deepest thanks to photographer Facundo Bustamante – I adore your images and the approach you take to your work – and to food stylist Pip Spence for your culinary skills and serenity. Max Robinson (prop stylist), Sara Vassallo (assistant food stylist) and Harry Brayne (assistant photographer) – you all helped make the shoot a success. I'm so proud to have had you all on the team.

Finally, thanks to Sophie, Sofie, Alicia, Katherine, Sarah and the whole gang at Quadrille for your support on this journey, and for bringing all the threads of the project together into such a beautiful, inspiring book. Once again, I'm very pleased to be part of the Quadrille family.

References

I'd like to acknowledge the following historical references I used in the introduction to this book:

An Economic History of Leftovers, The Atlantic, October 7 2015, by Helen Veit, associate professor of history at Michigan State University

The Curious History of Leftovers, History.com, November 20, 2018, by Natalia Mehlman Petrzela, associate professor of history at The New School

I also referred to the following in relation to food waste:

UK progress against Courtauld 2025 targets and UN Sustainable Development Goal 12.3

United Nations Environment Programme Food Waste Index Report 2021

Managing Director
Sarah Lavelle

Senior Commissioning Editor
Sophie Allen

Copy Editor
Stephanie Evans

Assistant Editor
Sofie Shearman

Designer
Alicia House

Photographer
Facundo Bustamante

Food Stylist
Pip Spence

Props Stylist
Max Robinson

Head of Production
Stephen Lang

Senior Production Controller
Katie Jarvis

First published in 2024 by Quadrille,
an imprint of Hardie Grant Publishing

Quadrille
52–54 Southwark Street
London SE1 1UN
quadrille.com

Text © Sue Quinn 2024
Photography © Facundo Bustamante 2024,
except for page 190 © Ruby Craig 2024
Design © Quadrille 2024

Cataloguing in Publication Data: a catalogue record for this book is
available from the British Library.

ISBN 978 1 83783 141 8
Printed in China